Layered Learning

Master Any Subject Faster, Crush Every Exam, and Retain Information Forever

Written and Published By: James Hernandez

James Hernandez

ISBN: 9798314516812

Imprint: Independently published

Layered Learning

Dedicated to my loving girlfriend, and to all of my family and friends who have helped me in so, so many ways. Whether you are young, old, sick, or healthy, you can always continue learning. You can continue growing.

James Hernandez

Table of Contents

Introduction: Why Most People Struggle with Studying

Most students are never taught *how* to study effectively, yet they are expected to figure it out on their own. In traditional education, "studying" often means re-reading textbooks, highlighting passages, and cramming the night before exams. These habits feel productive in the moment, but in reality they lead to disappointing results. Consider a common scenario: you spend hours diligently highlighting and reviewing a chapter, only to forget the majority of it by the next day. Or you recognize terms on a study guide and feel confident, but when you try to explain the concepts without looking, you blank out. These experiences illustrate core issues in our current approach to studying:

The Forgetting Curve

Without proper techniques, most of what we "learn" vanishes rapidly from memory. Psychologist Hermann Ebbinghaus famously showed that humans forget roughly 50% of new information within an hour and up to 70% within 24 hours if nothing is done to reinforce it. You might be shocked by how little you recall after so much effort.

Passive Learning Illusions

Methods like passive review and rote note-taking create an illusion of competence – we think we know the material because it looks familiar, when in fact we haven't truly mastered it. Re-reading notes or highlighted text makes content *feel* more obvious on each pass, which tricks the brain into feeling knowledgeable, even if we couldn't recall or apply that knowledge independently.

Overload and Burnout

Many students try to overcome poor retention by studying longer and longer, leading to marathon sessions that exhaust the brain. Ironically, after a certain point (around 3–4 hours of intense focus), putting in more time yields little to no benefit and can even be counterproductive. This information overload leads to mental fatigue – that feeling of your brain being "full" or that nothing is sticking anymore – and ultimately to burnout. Studying becomes unsustainable.

Why do these problems happen? Traditional study techniques don't align with how our brains actually learn. The human brain is not a tape recorder; it learns by actively engaging, connecting ideas, and periodically reinforcing information, not by passively absorbing it. When students only cram or re-read, they are writing knowledge "in sand" – easily washed away. They fall victim to the hidden curriculum of education, where critical learning strategies are never explicitly taught. This book aims to change that.

Imagine two students, Alice and Ben. Alice re-reads her notes and highlights her textbook in neon colors. Each pass makes the content seem more "obvious," lulling her into confidence. Ben, on the other hand, studies differently – he skims the chapter first to prime his brain, then creates a quick mind map of key ideas, and quizzes himself actively. He even tries teaching the concepts to an imaginary class. On test day, Alice is stunned that she doesn't recall details she *knows* she studied, while Ben effortlessly explains the answers. Stories like these are common; the difference is not IQ or effort, but strategy.

In this guide, we unveil a step-by-step learning framework that harnesses insights from cognitive science and proven techniques used by top learners. Drawing on research and advice from learning experts (and inspired by methods popularized by educators and authors in the field), each chapter will break down a crucial strategy – from layering knowledge and priming your brain, to visual mapping and advanced memory techniques – and show how it all fits together. You'll discover why each method works (the science), how to apply it (practical tips), real examples of success, links between strategies, and ways to avoid common pitfalls. By the end, you'll not only understand these techniques in theory, but will have experienced them through the very structure of this book. (In fact, this introduction is "priming" you – giving a big-picture preview – so your brain is ready to dive deeper in the upcoming chapters!)

Whether you're a college student aiming for higher grades, a high schooler learning how to learn, or a professional picking up new skills, the principles in this book will transform your approach. The journey ahead will first expose why our old study habits fail and then replace them with a science-backed system for mastering any subject. The difference is stark: doing well will no longer be about studying longer or harder but about studying *smarter* – in tune with the brain's natural learning processes.

Let's begin by understanding the problems with traditional studying, so we can then build a better way.

James Hernandez

Part 1: The Problems with Traditional Studying

One of the greatest challenges learners face is the rapid loss of new information, as our brains naturally discard details perceived as insignificant. Effective memory requires deep encoding through meaningful connections, context, and layered learning, simply memorizing isolated facts or cramming information quickly fades away. By replacing brute memorization with structured, active, and spaced approaches, students dramatically improve their ability to retain and recall information long-term.

Most students rely heavily on passive learning methods like rereading texts, highlighting, or mindlessly summarizing notes, which ends up creating an illusion of competence due to familiarity rather than true mastery. Research shows that these methods, though common, are largely ineffective for durable learning because they don't force active retrieval or deep processing. Passive techniques deceive learners and by introducing practical strategies such as active recall (self-testing), the Feynman Technique (teaching concepts simply), interactive highlighting (annotating with purpose), or converting notes into questions you can turn passive studying into active, meaningful engagement. Transitioning to these active methods leads to significantly improved understanding and lasting retention.

Many learners suffer from cognitive overload by attempting marathon study sessions, juggling excessive resources, or forcing themselves to digest huge volumes of information at once, leading to burnout and poor retention. Cognitive science reveals that the brain has a limited capacity (cognitive load) for absorbing new material effectively; after a certain point, additional studying becomes ineffective or even counterproductive. Adopting smarter, brain-friendly strategies ensures sustainable learning without sacrificing performance or well-being.

Students often mistake familiarity with true mastery, creating a dangerous "illusion of competence" where recognizing information feels like genuine knowledge, but they struggle when asked to recall or apply it independently. This cognitive bias, reinforced by passive study methods, leads learners to overestimate their understanding. Teaching material (even informally or imaginatively) actively counters this illusion by requiring deep processing, active recall, structured organization, and revealing gaps in knowledge. It introduces powerful methods like teaching imaginary students, peer-teaching in study groups, employing the Feynman Technique, and writing explanations for others. Ultimately, adopting the teacher mindset transforms surface familiarity into real mastery, exposing and filling gaps in knowledge and ensuring robust, reliable understanding.

Chapter 1: The Retention Crisis – Why We Forget What We Learn

One of the biggest challenges learners face is the rapid loss of new knowledge, often within days or even hours. As noted, without reinforcement we forget much of what we initially learn. Our brains are actually designed to forget; they filter out information that seems unimportant or unrelated to what we already know. This has survival benefits (we don't need to remember every trivial detail of our day), but it's a crisis for students trying to retain class material.

Why does forgetting happen so fast? Memory forms in stages. When you first encounter new information, it's held in short-term memory (like the RAM in a computer). To transfer it to long-term memory (where it can last days, months, or years), your brain needs to encode it deeply – by finding meaning, connecting it to existing knowledge, and revisiting it over time. Without these steps, new information remains fragile and fades quickly. Many students try to force memories by brute repetition or by memorizing facts in isolation, but without context or reinforcement, those facts never solidify. It's like pouring water into a leaky bucket: no matter how much you pour, it quickly drains away.

Another key issue is that the brain learns in layers, not all at once. We often overwhelm ourselves with details prematurely. Think of learning as building a brick wall: you need a foundation and structure before placing the small bricks. If you jump into memorizing minutiae (dates, formulas, definitions) without a "big picture" framework, those details have nothing to stick to – and thus slip away. Studies in cognitive psychology emphasize that meaningful organization of information greatly enhances retention. If the brain can attach a new fact to a broader concept or category, it's judged as more useful and stored more securely.

Practical Applications & Techniques

To tackle the retention crisis, we must work with our brain's tendencies. Here are some science-backed techniques to improve memory retention:

- **Preview and Contextualize (Priming):** Before diving into details, do a quick skim or overview of the material. This could mean reading the headings and summary of a chapter, or getting a sense of the main topics in a course. This primes your brain by providing context and signaling what's important. Like an advance organizer, it helps relate new ideas to what you already know, increasing retention. For example, before a lecture on photosynthesis, you might glance at a diagram of the process and note key terms (sunlight, chlorophyll, glucose). Later, when you learn the details, your brain will say, "aha, this fits into that process I saw earlier."

- **Encode in Layers:** Approach learning in multiple passes of increasing depth. First, focus on core principles and the logic behind the topic (the "foundation layer"). Next, add a layer of key concepts and relationships that build on those principles. Finally, include finer or more specific details (like examples, dates, exceptions). This *layered learning* method ensures each subsequent layer of information has a structure to anchor to. Learning experts champion this approach – for instance, one model outlines four layers of learning (basic logic, main concepts, important details, and fine details). By starting with a general understanding (the foundation), each new layer of detail can attach to something solid, drastically improving retention.

- **Active Encoding:** Don't just let information wash over you; engage with it as you learn. After reading a section or hearing a concept, pause and explain it in your own words (either aloud or in writing). This forces you to encode the idea deeply rather than relying on the author's phrasing. If you can't explain it clearly, that's a sign you haven't truly learned it yet. Creating a quick outline or a simple mind map of what you understood can also solidify the memory by giving it organization (more on visual mapping in a later chapter). The key is to process the information actively at the time of learning – summarize it, question it, teach it to your cat – rather than passively re-reading.

- **Spaced Reinforcement:** Perhaps the most powerful antidote to forgetting is to review the material multiple times over spaced intervals (we will explore this fully in the chapter on spaced repetition). For now, note that coming back to re-study or recall information the next day, then a few days later, then a week later, dramatically flattens the forgetting curve. Each review "refills the leaky bucket" and strengthens memory, so you lose information much more slowly. For example, instead of reading something once and moving on, revisit it briefly the next morning and again next week – each review will help lock it in.

Consider two students in a history class learning about World War II. Student A reads the chapter once on Sunday and again on Monday, highlighting key dates and names both times. Student B spends that same total time differently: on Sunday she skims the chapter headings (priming) and then writes a one-page summary of the causes and major events from memory (active encoding). She also glances at a timeline of WWII to frame the events (Layer 1: the big-picture chronology). On Monday, she reads the full chapter and adds details to her summary in the appropriate places (Layer 2: key details plugged into the timeline). Over the next week, Student B quickly reviews her one-page summary twice (spaced reinforcement). Come exam day a month later, Student B recalls the sequence of events and critical details with ease. Student A, who simply re-read the text in a block, struggles to recall facts out of context. Student B's layered, active approach gave her brain meaningful connections (a timeline framework) and repeated exposure over time, solving the retention problem.

Connections Between Methods

The strategies previewed here connect to many techniques we'll discuss in detail later. For instance, priming (Chapter 5) and pre-testing (Chapter 9) are ways to get that initial exposure that combats forgetting. Mind mapping (Chapter 8) is a method of organizing information visually, which essentially creates layers of knowledge and context –

improving retention by linking ideas together. And of course, spaced repetition (Chapter 13) directly addresses the forgetting curve by optimally timing your reviews. As you progress through the book, you'll see these threads come up again and again: organize information, engage actively, and revisit periodically. These are the three pillars to defeating the retention crisis.

Common Misconceptions & How to Overcome Them

A common misconception is "If I understand it now, I'll remember it later." In reality, recognizing information at study time does not guarantee you'll recall it in the future. Recognizing your notes or textbook examples is easier because the information is right in front of you, giving your brain lots of cues. But in an exam (or any real situation), you often have to retrieve the information without those cues. **To overcome this:** constantly test yourself without looking at the material. Self-quizzing ensures you can recall knowledge in the absence of hints, which is the true test of memory.

Another misconception: "Repeating something often enough in one sitting means it will stick." While brute-force repetition can help short-term recall, it's highly inefficient for long-term memory. Ten exposures in one day are not as effective as those same ten exposures spread over several days. **Overcome this false belief** by restructuring your study schedule: plan multiple short review sessions instead of one big cram session. By spacing out your practice (even by a day or two), you give your brain time to begin forgetting and then strengthen the memory when you recall it again.

Finally, some believe "Memory fades inevitably, there's nothing you can do about it." On the contrary, memory can be trained. By applying the methods above – spacing your reviews, actively recalling information, building knowledge in layers – students have dramatically improved their retention. For example, introducing frequent self-quizzes and spaced reviews in a class setting led to drastic improvements in exam performance compared to classes that relied on last-minute cramming. The key is knowing *how* to work with your memory. And that knowledge is exactly what this book provides.

Chapter 2: Passive Learning – The Trap of Rereading, Highlighting, and Summarizing

Think about the go-to study habits of most students: reading and re-reading notes or textbooks, highlighting important sentences, and maybe writing summaries or copying definitions onto flashcards. These are *passive* learning techniques – you're consuming information without actively retrieving or applying it. Research has shown that such methods are among the least effective for true learning. Why? Because they create an *illusion* of learning without much substance.

When you re-read a chapter, the text becomes familiar, and your brain often misinterprets that familiarity as "I know this now." This phenomenon is part of the illusion of competence: we equate familiarity with mastery. Psychologists have found that people are poor judges of their own learning – we tend to feel more confident if information is right in front of us or if we *just* saw it, but that confidence doesn't necessarily reflect what we can recall unaided. Highlighting, similarly, makes us feel like we're distilling key points, but often students end up with swaths of neon text without deeper processing. The act of highlighting is itself too easy; it doesn't require truly understanding the material, only identifying it as "something to remember." As one educational review bluntly put it, a great deal of research demonstrates that common techniques such as highlighting, re-reading, and mindlessly copying notes are largely ineffectual when used in isolation – they just don't lead to durable learning.

Summarizing or re-writing notes can be more engaging than re-reading, but many students do it mindlessly – essentially transcribing the textbook in slightly shorter form. If you find yourself copying sentences verbatim or just rearranging phrases, you're not forcing your brain to grapple with the concepts. It's possible to write pages of notes and still not be able to explain the content or answer questions on it, as some unhappy test-takers discover.

Why are these techniques so popular if they're ineffective? Firstly, they are low-effort and give a quick sense of accomplishment – it's easy to convince yourself you "studied" when you spent two hours reading or produced a stack of highlighted pages or rewritten notes. Secondly, the immediate feedback is deceiving: right after re-reading, you recognize the material and it *feels* like it's clicking. But that's because your brain is seeing it in the same context with all cues present (recognition), not because you could recall it on your own (recall). True learning requires being able to summon information *out of context*, like on a blank page or a tough exam question. Passive techniques don't train that ability.

Practical Applications & Techniques

To escape the passive learning trap, we need to turn passive tasks into active ones:

- **Active Recall over Rereading:** Instead of reading a chapter three times, read it once *actively*: pause periodically and quiz yourself on what you remember so far. Close the book and recite or write down the main ideas from that section. If you're studying slides or notes, cover them and try to rewrite the key points from memory. Only re-read to check what you missed or got wrong. This approach harnesses the "testing effect" – the finding that actively recalling information strengthens memory more than repeated exposure. For example, if you need to learn a biological process, attempt to draw it out from memory rather than tracing it from the textbook. By forcing your brain to retrieve the information, you solidify the memory.

- **The Feynman Technique:** Named after Nobel-winning physicist Richard Feynman, this is a form of active note-taking and self-explanation. Take a concept you're learning and write an explanation of it as if you were teaching a complete beginner (say, a 12-year-old child). Use simple language and even analogies. This forces you to truly understand the concept in order to simplify it. Any point where you struggle to explain or find yourself resorting to copying the textbook's wording highlights a gap in your understanding – that's where you should focus your studying. This technique turns summarizing into an active exercise and exposes the illusion of competence because if you *thought* you understood something but can't explain it simply, you haven't mastered it yet.

- **Interactive Highlighting:** If you do use highlighting, make it an *interactive* process. Don't mark a passage unless you also annotate *why* it's important or how it connects to a larger idea. For instance, highlight a definition, but in the margin jot a quick note or question about it ("How does this concept relate to X we learned earlier?"). This way, highlighting isn't an endpoint but a starting point for deeper thinking. Another tip: consider highlighting on a second pass rather than the first read. For example, read a section and quiz yourself first; then highlight the parts you found were truly key when you tried to recall. That way the highlighted portions are vetted by your own recall process as essential points.

- **Replace Passive Review with Active Review:** Instead of reading your notes over and over, transform them into something you *do*. One method is to convert your notes into a series of questions (this is the essence of the Recall-Question Method popularized by some study experts). Each bullet point in your notes becomes a prompt: e.g., turn "Definition: mitosis = cell division that results in two identical daughter cells" into the question "What is mitosis and what does it produce?" Now when you review, you're *answering* those questions, not just glazing over statements. This small change turns passive note-review into an active quiz. Similarly, if you have a set of highlighted sentences, you can make each into a question and quiz yourself, or cover up sections of your summary and attempt to rewrite them from memory.

A famous experiment on learning strategies compared students who repeatedly re-read a passage with students who read it once and then tried to recall it from memory. Initially, after studying, the re-readers felt more confident and even performed slightly better on an *immediate* test. But when tested a week later, the roles reversed: the recall-practice group remembered far more. This shows how passive review can inflate short-term performance (and confidence) but fails in long-term retention. The act of recall, even with initial errors, dramatically improved memory after a delay.

Dr. Cal Newport, in his book *How to Become a Straight-A Student*, noted that many top students avoid rote review entirely. Cal himself, when he started college, initially used elaborate highlighting systems, thinking that would distill the material. Later, he discovered that active recall was far superior – he would read a chapter *once*, then close the book and *recite* the key ideas or teach them to himself, only referring back to the text to check accuracy. He found this mentally taxing at first, but it "astonishingly improved information retention" and even felt like it gave him a near photographic memory for exam material. The takeaway: students who ditch pure rereading in favor of self-testing often see dramatic improvements in both understanding and grades.

Even in everyday studying, small shifts make a big difference. Let's say James has to memorize the anatomy of the human heart:

- **Method 1 (passive):** He reads the chapter and highlights each part of the heart in the diagram, then re-reads his highlighted notes.

- **Method 2 (active):** He looks at the heart diagram, covers the labels, and tests himself on naming each part; he then explains to himself how blood flows through the heart, step by step, without looking. When he gets stuck, he peeks at the book, then tries again.

It's easy to guess who will perform better on the anatomy quiz: James in Method 2 will likely recall the heart's structure much more vividly than if he had only passively reviewed it. By testing himself and explaining the process, he created strong mental links and identified his weak spots early.

Connections Between Methods

The pitfalls of passive learning underscore the importance of the active methods discussed throughout this book. For instance, *Active Recall* (Chapter 6) is essentially the cure for passive review – in Chapter 6 we'll explore in depth why and how actively retrieving information is the "#1 strategy" for learning efficiently. Similarly, *Mind Mapping* (Chapter 8) can replace passive note-taking with a more active, brain-friendly approach: instead of copying linear notes, you build a web of connections as you create a mind map, which forces you to think about how pieces fit together. Even *Interleaving* (Chapter 12) connects here: switching between topics or problem types keeps your practice active and prevents the autopilot mode that passive studying often encourages. When you interleave different kinds of problems, you can't just memorize one procedure and coast; you have to actively think about which strategy to use for each problem, thereby avoiding passivity.

Common Misconceptions & How to Overcome Them

Perhaps the most pernicious misconception is "If I spend a long time studying, I'll learn it – *how* I study doesn't matter as much as putting in the hours." Students often equate hours of effort with effectiveness, which leads many to persist with rereading or highlighting simply because they're clocking time. To overcome this, one must internalize that effective studying is about *cognitive engagement*, not just time spent. Ten hours of passive review may feel responsible or reassuring, but as research shows, it can be largely wasted time. It's better to spend, say, six hours actively testing yourself and questioning the material – your brain will actually retain more in less total time. In short, don't measure your study by hours or pages; measure it by how many times you actively recalled or applied the information.

Another misconception: "Writing notes or summaries is automatically helpful." Writing can be helpful, *if* the act of writing involves processing the information (for example, putting things in your own words or reorganizing ideas). But if you simply copy text or take down notes verbatim without processing, it's not much better than reading passively. **Overcome this** by always checking yourself: after writing a summary, close the original source and see if you can explain the idea just from your summary notes. If your summary is mostly copied phrases or if you still can't explain it without looking back at the textbook, you need to refine your approach – perhaps by using the Feynman Technique or by reorganizing the information into questions or a concept map. The goal is that the act of note-taking itself engages your brain; if it doesn't, change how you're doing it.

Some students believe "I have a bad memory, so I need to keep reading it again and again." Often, it's not your memory that's bad – it's the method. By embracing active techniques, even those who thought they were "slow learners" often find they remember much more. For instance, one student in a nursing program lamented on a forum that highlighting and rereading weren't helping her retain anything for her exams. An experienced peer suggested doing practice quizzes and trying to teach the concepts to a friend. The student was amazed at how much more she recalled after just a couple of weeks of weekly self-quizzing and explaining concepts out loud, compared to her old nightly rereads. Her memory wasn't the issue – the strategy was.

In summary, passive studying is a comfortable but deceptive zone that holds learners back. Breaking out of it may feel challenging at first – active learning is more demanding and can expose what you don't know (which can be humbling). But the payoff is huge: not only will you remember more, you'll truly understand the material and be able to apply it. In the upcoming chapters, we will reinforce this shift by focusing on active recall and other high-utility techniques – effectively replacing those old passive habits with powerful new ones backed by cognitive science.

Chapter 3: Overload & Burnout – Too Much Information, Not Enough Absorption

Scientific Explanations

Modern learners often face an information overload. With syllabi packed full of topics, endless online resources, and the pressure to excel, students tend to respond by trying to study *everything* for long hours. It's common to hear of all-night study sessions or 8-hour library marathons. Unfortunately, the brain has limits on how much it can absorb at once. Cognitive science describes a concept called *cognitive load* – essentially, the amount of working memory resources needed to understand material. When cognitive load is too high (for example, when the material is very dense and we try to consume a lot of it quickly), learning efficiency plummets. You may experience this as the sensation of your "brain being full" or that nothing is sticking after a certain point.

Research on practice habits suggests there are diminishing returns after a few hours of intense study in a day. In fact, classic studies in psychology found little to no benefit from practice beyond about 4 hours per day, and reduced benefits beyond about 2 hours – beyond these durations, fatigue and mental saturation kick in, making additional study time far less effective. Think of your brain like a sponge: it can only hold so much water at once. Past saturation, any extra water (information) just drips away without being retained. Yet many students, fearing they haven't done enough, keep pouring in more study time, leading to exhaustion without better learning.

Another factor is *relevance and interest.* The brain naturally prioritizes information that it deems important or relevant. If you're trying to force yourself to learn a deluge of facts that you find meaningless, your brain's retention will be low – it's inclined to dump that info as "not useful." This ties into motivation and curiosity. Neuroscience research has shown that when our curiosity is aroused, the hippocampus (a key memory center) becomes more receptive, and we retain not just the interesting information but even incidental information better. In one study, participants rated their curiosity about various trivia questions; when their curiosity was high, they not only learned the answers better but also remembered unrelated content presented in between. The takeaway: interest acts like a turbo-boost for memory. Conversely, when we're bored or overwhelmed, our brain's "save" button works poorly.

So, in an overload situation – too much material, not enough time – simply grinding for more hours is not the answer. It often leads to burnout: mental exhaustion, loss of motivation, and even anxiety or dislike for the subject. Burnout further impedes learning by reducing concentration and creative thinking. Students in burnout mode often read pages without processing them (ever find you read a paragraph and immediately realized you didn't absorb a word? That's cognitive overload at work).

Practical Applications & Techniques

How can we study *smarter*, not harder, when confronted with a huge volume of material? Here are strategies to avoid overload and burnout:

- **Prioritize and Use the Pareto Principle:** Embrace the idea that not all information is equally important. Use the 80/20 rule (Pareto principle) – identify the 20% of the content that is likely to yield 80% of the value or that is fundamental to understanding the rest. In a textbook chapter, for instance, there may be a few key concepts that everything else builds upon. Focus on truly mastering those first. Often, learning those core ideas makes the smaller details easier to remember because you can attach them to the core framework. Ask your instructor (or look at past exams) to figure out what the big-ticket items are. By prioritizing, you reduce overload and ensure you're spending energy on what matters most.

- **Curiosity-Driven Sequencing:** If possible, start your study session with the topic that interests you most. This might sound counterintuitive (many assume you should tackle the hardest or dullest stuff first), but beginning with something engaging can ignite your overall curiosity about the subject. That heightened interest can carry over and make the less exciting parts a bit more palatable. Moreover, once you grasp an interesting facet of a subject, you often gain more context to understand the "drier" bits. For example, if a physics student is fascinated by black holes but dreads the math of general relativity, reading a captivating article or watching a short video on black hole phenomena *first* might motivate her and provide context that makes slogging through the equations more meaningful. The idea is to make learning an adventure of discovery, not just a chore. By allowing yourself to follow your curiosity (at least initially), you engage the brain's reward system. This can combat feelings of overload because genuine interest gives you mental energy.

- **Chunking and Breaks:** Break study material into bite-sized "chunks." Instead of a 4-hour continuous block to cover three chapters, break it into, say, 8 sessions of 30 minutes each (or whatever duration you can maintain focus), each focused on a manageable section or concept, with short breaks in between sessions. During breaks, do something different – walk around, stretch, grab a snack, let your mind rest. These pauses help reset your cognitive load. When you return, you'll find it easier to focus and integrate the next chunk of material. Studies on learning and work productivity show that periodic breaks actually improve overall output and retention (this is part of why techniques like the Pomodoro Technique – typically 25 minutes study, 5 minutes break – are popular). Your brain uses the downtime to subconsciously consolidate what you just learned, and you come back refreshed.

- **Organize to Combat Overwhelm:** Feeling overwhelmed often comes from viewing the material as an amorphous mass of facts. Employ organizing tools like outlines or mind maps to create structure for the content *before* you fully learn everything. If you lay out the skeleton of the topic – main headings, sub-points, relationships – you give your brain a scaffold to hold on to. This reduces the sense of "too much at once," because you can tackle one part of the scaffold at a time. For instance, before studying a 100-page unit, spend some time constructing a one-page overview of the unit's structure (drawn from the table of contents or chapter summaries). This external organization unloads some cognitive burden because you don't have to hold the entire map of the content in your head while studying – it's on paper. (As we'll see later, "externalizing" knowledge into a visual form frees mental resources for learning the details, and helps you see connections that make those details more memorable.)

- **Set Limits and Schedule Downtime:** Prevent burnout by scheduling clear cut-off times for studying each day and making sure you have leisure or rest activities. Your brain needs recovery. Ironically, stepping away from studies to exercise or sleep can sometimes do more for your learning than an extra hour of cramming. Sleep, in particular, is when a lot of memory consolidation happens – pulling an all-nighter can seriously impair your ability to retain what you studied and reduce your cognitive performance the next day. So, plan your study in a way that you can sleep adequately, especially before an exam. Trust the science that beyond a certain point, rest will serve you better than more grinding. Giving yourself permission to relax isn't wasting time; it's an investment in productivity.

- **Limit Excess Resources:** In the age of the internet, another form of overload is using too many sources. Some students think "more sources = better understanding," so they pile on textbooks, YouTube lectures, and reference articles – soon they're drowning in information from all sides. While cross-referencing can help if your main source is unclear, too many sources can cause confusion and overwhelm (you might encounter conflicting info or just be buried by volume). The solution is to pick one or two good resources for core learning and use additional sources sparingly for clarification on specific points. It's perfectly fine to limit your scope – mastering one well-chosen textbook or set of notes is better than skimming three different sources and mastering none.

Ultimately, to beat overload and burnout, one must tune into how the brain works best: in focused bursts, with rest, and driven by meaning and interest. Study can and should be sustainable. In the next part of the book, we will equip you with specific scientific techniques (like priming, active recall, and spacing) that inherently make studying more efficient and manageable – effectively guarding you against overload by design. As you apply them, you'll find you can learn more in less total time and with far less stress.

Chapter 4: The Illusion of Competence – Why Recognizing Information Isn't Mastery

Scientific Explanations

Have you ever read through your notes and thought, "Yep, I know this, I know this..." – but when the test (or a real challenge) comes, you struggle to recall or apply the knowledge? This is the illusion of competence in action. It's a cognitive bias where learners overestimate their understanding or memory of a topic simply because it *feels* familiar or easy in the moment of studying. A classic scenario: reading the solution to a problem and thinking "I would have gotten that," or nodding along to an explained concept and assuming you understand it fully. However, recognition is not the same as recall or true understanding. Recognizing information (seeing something and thinking "oh yeah, that looks familiar") is a much shallower process than being able to retrieve it on your own or explain it from scratch.

Cognitive psychologists such as Koriat and Bjork have studied how learners judge their own knowledge, and they found systematic errors. For example, when the cue or context is present (like seeing a question and its answer together, or having the textbook in front of you), learners tend to think they would remember it later. But when tested without the answer visible or the notes handy, they often cannot produce it. This is sometimes called *foresight bias* – we're bad at predicting our future performance after a delay, especially when we base it on how things feel during study. Another aspect is *fluency*: if something is presented in a fluent, easy-to-digest way (like a well-written textbook explanation or a charismatic lecture), we can mistake that fluency for our own mastery. "It made so much sense when I read it" – yes, because the author or instructor did the thinking for you. Real competence means you can do the thinking or recall the information *unaided*.

Illusions of competence are reinforced by passive study techniques (as discussed in Chapter 2). Highlighting a sentence and then later seeing that neon marker gives a false sense of "importance registered." Re-reading notes that you yourself wrote can make you feel "I remember writing this," but do you remember the content itself, or just the act of writing? Familiarity with the page or the phrasing can trick you.

They say the best way to learn something is to teach it – and there's truth to that. This ties into what's known as the *protégé effect* or "learning-by-teaching." Studies have found that when learners expect to teach material to someone else, they learn it more effectively and organize it better in their minds. When you teach or even simply explain a concept (whether to an actual person or just out loud to yourself), several beneficial things happen that counter illusions of knowing:

- **Active Recall and Elaboration:** Teaching forces you to retrieve information from memory and explain it in your own words, which is active recall, and to elaborate on it (creating connections or analogies so someone else can understand). Research supports this: in one experiment, students who *expected* to have to teach recalled more key points and structured their recall more coherently than those who expected just a test. That's because while teaching, you naturally impose structure and emphasis – you identify what's important (to stress it to the learner) and link concepts logically to explain them clearly. In other words, teaching makes you mentally organize the material and articulate the logic, preventing the illusion that you know it when you've only followed someone else's organized explanation.

- **Exposure of Gaps:** When you try to teach something, any area you don't fully understand will quickly become evident – you'll stumble in your explanation, or your "student" might ask a question you can't answer, or you'll realize you skipped a step you can't explain. This immediate feedback (even if it's just *you* noticing "hmm, I can't explain this part well") tells you exactly where your knowledge is shaky, so you can reinforce it. It's far better to discover these gaps in a low-stakes teaching practice than during a high-stakes exam. Essentially, teaching forces true understanding because you cannot gloss over a point without noticing that you don't get it when you have to articulate it.

- **Improved Memory Encoding:** Explaining aloud engages more senses and thought processes than silent reading or thinking. You hear yourself speak, you might see diagrams or gestures you produce while explaining, and you're processing ideas verbally. This multi-modal encoding creates more retrieval cues later on. Additionally, by teaching, you often turn the information into a narrative or logical flow ("first this happens, then that, because…"), which our brains find easier to remember than disjointed facts. In short, teaching a topic not only highlights what you don't know, it also solidifies what you *do* know by encoding it more richly.

- **Confidence and Motivation:** As you successfully teach and clarify concepts (even if just to yourself), you build confidence in your mastery. This positive feeling can reduce anxiety and improve performance in actual tests, with the logic: "I explained this to someone; I must understand it well enough to handle exam questions." Additionally, knowing you will teach someone can be motivating to study – you don't want to let your "student" down, so you prepare more thoroughly. That motivation factor was noted in research: just the expectation of teaching made students adopt more effective study strategies spontaneously. In a way, anticipating the responsibility of teaching makes you more accountable to truly learn the material.

- **Relational and Big-Picture Thinking:** Good teaching tends to focus on the relationships between ideas ("this leads to that because…", "this concept is similar to that concept in the previous chapter…"). By doing so, you solidify how pieces of knowledge fit together, which is a higher-order level of understanding. It moves you beyond rote recall of isolated facts to seeing the system or framework connecting them, which yields better transfer of knowledge to new problems. Essentially, explaining a concept to someone often forces you to see the big picture and the logical structure, further combating any illusion that knowing terms equals understanding the subject.

One interesting phenomenon is that when learners explain something, they sometimes fill in logical gaps in their knowledge by reasoning them out on the spot. This relates to the Feynman Technique: in trying to explain simply, you might realize "Oh, I never learned why X happens, let me try to deduce it…" – and you end up bridging the gap through reasoning, thereby truly learning it. So, teaching not only reveals gaps, it can also help you *bridge* those gaps through the very act of trying to explain (learning in real-time as you teach).

Practical Applications & Techniques

You don't need a formal classroom to harness teaching as a learning tool. Here's how to do it:

- **Teach an Imaginary Class (or a Rubber Duck):** This might sound quirky but explaining out loud to an empty room or even to a rubber duck (a famous technique in programming for debugging) can be very effective. After studying a chapter or concept, pretend you have a student (perhaps imagine your younger sibling or just an attentive audience) and explain the material from start to finish, aloud and in a clear way. Simplify where possible, as if you're teaching a novice. The act of vocalizing will force clarity of thought. If you stumble or get confused at any point, mark that part for review – that's an indication you didn't fully understand it. You can even anticipate questions your imaginary student might ask ("Why does that happen?" or "Can you give an example?") and make sure you can answer them. This method lets you practice teaching without any judgment from others. It's just you and perhaps a stuffed animal, but it effectively surfaces whether you really grasp the material.

- **Study Groups & Peer Teaching:** Join or form a small study group where each member agrees to "teach" certain topics to the others. For example, if you have four chapters to cover, each person can prepare to explain one chapter to the group for 10-15 minutes while the others listen and ask questions. The process of preparing to teach ensures you learn your portion thoroughly. Meanwhile, as a listener, you might get a fresh perspective or new mnemonics from your peer's explanation. Encourage questions when you're the teacher – your peers' questions will often highlight nuances or missing pieces in your explanation, reinforcing your understanding when you clarify or discuss the answers. Even the expectation of having to teach your peers can improve how you initially study (you might make mental "lesson plans" or think of analogies in advance). So, schedule rotating teaching sessions in your group; knowing "next Monday I'm teaching Chapter 3" will prime you to study it more actively beforehand.

- **Feynman Technique:** Richard Feynman, the famous physicist, used a method to learn anything by explaining it in the simplest terms possible. The steps are: Pick a concept, study it, then write out (or speak) an explanation as if teaching a child or someone with no background. Use simple language and analogies; avoid jargon. When you get to a part you can't explain simply or you have to use complex terms you don't really understand, that signals a gap. Go back to the source material, learn that part better, and then refine your explanation. Repeat until you can explain the entire concept in basic terms, coherently and clearly. This is like teaching on paper (or to an imaginary young student). It's powerful because it forces you to confront complexity and distill it, which means you must deeply understand it. That simple explanation you produce becomes a mental anchor: if you can tell the "story" of the concept in simple terms, you likely grasp it thoroughly. You can also do this step by step aloud: "Okay, how would I explain this idea to a kid? Let me try…"

- **Tutor Someone Else:** If feasible, actually tutor a friend or someone in a lower level of the course. For example, help a classmate who is struggling, or a younger student who is learning the subject you've already taken. Teaching them the fundamentals will reinforce your own understanding, and their questions or mistakes can give you new perspectives or reveal assumptions you didn't realize you had. Even tutoring material you think you know well often solidifies the core knowledge and sometimes shows edge-cases you hadn't considered. Many graduate students mention that teaching undergraduate courses or labs made them *truly* master their own undergraduate content. If you don't have a formal tutoring setup, you could offer to explain a tough concept to a study buddy in exchange for them explaining another concept to you – a mutual teach-back arrangement.

- **Teach in Writing (Blogs, Study Forums):** If you enjoy writing, try explaining concepts on paper or online. For instance, answer questions on a forum (like Stack Exchange for academic subjects) or write a short blog post/tutorial on something you've learned. Writing forces you to be clear and precise (similar to speaking, but you can refine your wording). Suppose you just mastered a tricky concept in economics; you might write a post titled "In simple terms: How supply and demand create market equilibrium." To write it understandably, you have to make sure you get it right and communicate clearly. Others might comment if something is unclear or ask follow-up questions, which further refines your understanding. This approach not only reinforces your knowledge, but if you can teach strangers on the internet an idea successfully, you definitely know it.

- **Pretend to Be the Teacher on the Exam:** A fun twist while studying is to create potential exam questions (and model answers) as if you were the instructor. By doing this, you put yourself in the teacher's shoes. Coming up with a good test question requires understanding what the key learning points are and how to probe them. It also makes you consider common pitfalls or tricky angles. For example, after studying a chapter, write 3-5 possible exam questions covering the main ideas and then write what an ideal answer would include. In doing so, you effectively teach via the exam format. Later, see if those or similar questions appear on the real exam – even if they don't, the exercise will have ensured you covered the main ideas thoroughly (and you might have anticipated the actual questions' topics).

- **Use Visual Aids in Your Explanations:** When you teach (even to yourself), draw diagrams or write on a whiteboard or scratch paper as if you were giving a lecture. Teaching is often enhanced with visuals, and the ability to produce a diagram from memory is itself a sign of mastery. If you can illustrate a process (like sketching the steps of cell division or drawing a timeline of historical events) and talk through it coherently, you're encoding the information both visually and verbally. Also, this brings in the mind mapping or note skills from earlier chapters: for example, you might say, "Let me draw a quick mind map to show how these concepts connect." Doing so from scratch during your explanation is a powerful combination of active recall and teaching.

- **Be Mindful of the "Illusion of Teaching":** Usually, teaching others is one of the best tests of knowledge, but there's a possible pitfall: it's conceivable to teach something incorrectly or incompletely and not realize it, especially if your "student" doesn't know enough to question you. This could give you false confidence ("I explained it, so I must understand it"). To avoid this, after you teach, do a self-check: revisit the source or notes to ensure your explanation was accurate and complete. Usually, teaching will highlight the gaps, but you want to verify you didn't accidentally reinforce a misunderstanding with a slick but flawed explanation. In short, teaching is a great tool, but double-check that what you taught is correct – that final verification will eliminate any lingering illusions.

In one study, one group of students was told they would have to teach the material to other students after learning it, and another group was told they'd be tested on it. In reality, all students were tested. The group that prepared to teach not only remembered more, but their recall was better organized and they answered more main-point questions correctly. They studied differently – making sure they understood deeply and could articulate the logic, rather than just memorizing facts. This demonstrates that even if you don't actually end up teaching someone, adopting the *mindset* of a teacher shifts how you learn (you might create mental "lesson plans" or think of analogies as you study, which helps).

Anecdotally, consider a story of a medical student who formed a study group where each member regularly did a brief "teach-back" of assigned topics (essentially mini-lectures) to the others. He found that when it was his turn to teach a topic, he learned it far more comprehensively beforehand – and when listening, he could gauge how well his peers had mastered their topics. By the time exams came, every member had effectively taught and been taught each major topic, and they all performed excellently. He credited the peer-teaching approach for eliminating any weak spots in understanding.

Part 2: The Science of Efficient Learning

Now that we've identified the major pitfalls of traditional studying (forgetting, passivity, overload, and illusions of knowing), we turn to solutions. In Part 2, we shift to specific techniques that make learning more effective and efficient. Each of these strategies is grounded in cognitive science and is designed to align your study habits with how your brain learns best. We'll cover methods like priming (preparing your brain before deep study), active recall (the powerhouse retrieval practice), layering information, visual mapping of ideas, and pre-testing. Each chapter in this part introduces one of these core techniques, explaining why it works and how to apply it. By using them, you will inherently organize your learning, stay mentally engaged, and reinforce your memory over time – in other words, you'll study *smarter*. Let's dive into the first of these strategies: priming your brain for learning success.

Chapter 5: The Priming Effect – Preparing the Brain for Learning Success

Scientific Explanations

Before learning any new topic in depth, there's a powerful psychological technique that can boost your understanding and retention: priming. In the context of learning, *priming* means giving your brain a preview or introduction to the material before you fully tackle it. This could be as simple as skimming a chapter, reviewing the learning objectives, or looking at key diagrams and headings. Why does this matter? Because the brain is a pattern-seeking organ – it learns new information by connecting it with what it already knows. Priming essentially "warms up" the relevant neural circuits and provides a mental framework or set of "slots" into which new details can fit.

Imagine your brain as a puzzle board. Trying to learn something cold (with no priming) is like dumping out puzzle pieces without knowing what the final picture looks like – you can still assemble it with effort, but it's harder and takes longer. Priming is like looking at the puzzle box cover first: you see the big picture, so when you handle each piece, you have context for where it might go. Educational psychologist David Ausubel's theory of *advance organizers* (dating back to the 1960s) showed that giving learners a high-level overview or analogy *before* learning detailed content significantly increased retention and understanding. The advance organizer acts as a mental hook for the details to come.

Priming works by leveraging prior knowledge and curiosity. Even if you know nothing about a topic, a brief skim can activate related knowledge. For example, you might not know neuroscience yet, but skimming a chapter about "memory formation" might trigger thoughts of things you *do* know ("oh, hippocampus – I've heard that word"; "sleep and memory, I recall something about that"). Those little connections get your neurons ready to latch onto new info. Also, seeing intriguing headings or questions raises questions in your mind, creating an information gap your brain now wants to fill. This is related to the *curiosity effect*: when you have questions, your brain becomes more receptive to answers.

Moreover, priming addresses cognitive load. When you jump into complex material with no preparation, you're simultaneously trying to grasp basic terms and high-level ideas all at once, which is overwhelming. Priming separates these tasks: first you get the lay of the land and basic vocabulary, so when you dive deeper, your mind isn't completely swamped with *all* new everything. It's already somewhat organized. One could say priming activates "schema" or mental categories that incoming information can attach to, reducing the cognitive effort during learning.

In essence, priming is like preparing soil before planting seeds: it creates a fertile ground for knowledge to take root. By giving your brain context and a heads-up about what's coming, you help it allocate attention properly and form initial connections that will later support detailed memory.

Practical Applications & Techniques

Priming is one of the easiest techniques to implement, yet it yields disproportionate benefits. Here are practical ways to prime your brain before learning:

- **Pre-Read/Skim the Material:** Spend 5–10 minutes skimming a textbook chapter or article before you study it in detail. Look at section headings, subheadings, any bold or italicized terms, summaries, and diagrams or tables. Don't worry about fully understanding everything in this skim; your goal is just to acquaint yourself with the general ideas and terminology. For example, if you're about to read a chapter on Photosynthesis, skim and note that it has sections on "Light Reactions" and "Calvin Cycle," and it mentions terms like ATP, chlorophyll, CO_2, etc. Even if those terms are fuzzy to you, your brain now has a checklist of "things that will appear." When you later read in detail, you'll recognize these terms ("Oh right, this was mentioned in that diagram") – and recognition combined with context leads to better memory. **Key tip:** After skimming, try to predict or outline what you think the chapter will cover. For instance, you might think, "This looks like it will explain how plants convert sunlight into chemical energy, probably covering what happens in chloroplasts." Even if your prediction isn't perfectly accurate, the act of guessing sets up a mental scaffold and piques your curiosity ("I wonder if I'm right?"), which keeps you alert during the actual study.

- **Identify 3–5 Core Concepts or Questions:** Before starting a new lecture or unit, quickly ask yourself: "What do I think are the main ideas here?" If you have learning objectives provided, read them. If not, make an educated guess from the topic title. For example, if the lecture is on "Quantum Mechanics – Introduction," you might guess key concepts like "particle-wave duality," "Heisenberg uncertainty principle," etc., or simply note questions like "What are the fundamental principles of quantum mechanics?" If you're not sure, ask "What do I want to learn or clarify from this?" and jot those down. By doing this, you prime your focus. As you study, you'll naturally be looking to answer those questions or confirm if those concepts are indeed important, which keeps your engagement high.

- **Glossary Check:** If the material has many new terms (common in sciences, technical subjects, or even humanities readings heavy with new jargon), take a moment to glance through a glossary or list of key terms first. Learn just a one-line definition or category for each unfamiliar term. Think of it as meeting the "cast of characters" before reading a novel. You don't need each term in depth, just a basic idea of what it is. For instance, before diving into a chapter on cellular respiration, if you quickly note: "ATP – energy molecule," "mitochondria – organelle where it happens," "NADH – electron carrier," then when you read the process, you won't stumble over those terms; you already know who's who at a superficial level. This lets you follow the story instead of pausing at each unknown word.

- **Use a Mind Map or Outline as a "Blueprint":** You can enhance priming by creating a quick mind map or outline of what you *think* the structure is, based on your skim. In the center of a page, write the central topic, and branch out main subtopics (maybe drawn from headings you saw or just your initial understanding). It's okay if this initial map is incomplete or partly guesswork. It serves as your advance organizer. As you learn, you'll fill it in or correct it. The very act of sketching this out is a strong primer in itself – you've essentially hypothesized the structure of the knowledge, which primes your brain to verify and adjust that structure while studying. It's akin to an engineer reviewing blueprints before constructing a building; you're giving your brain a blueprint of the topic.

- **Brief Pre-lecture Research:** If you know tomorrow's class is about, say, "The French Revolution," spending 10 minutes the night before reading the Wikipedia summary or a short introductory article can prime you to get much more out of the actual lecture. You'll walk into class already knowing the basic timeline and key figures, so the professor's deeper discussion finds "ready soil" in your mind. This is especially useful for classes where lectures can be dense or fast-paced – a bit of pre-reading prevents that lost feeling because you have some context. Essentially, you're turning the lecture into a reinforcement rather than your first encounter with the material.

- **Mental Activation – Recall Prior Knowledge:** Before learning something new, take a moment to ask yourself, "What do I already know about this topic, or something related?" Even if it's fragmentary, recalling any related knowledge primes relevant neural connections. Suppose you're about to learn about supply and demand in economics; you might think, "I've heard that when supply goes up, prices go down... there's something about equilibrium too." Just that recollection means when you study it properly, that prior idea will link up with the detailed explanation, reinforcing your memory. This is why teachers often start by saying, "Remember last week's topic X? It relates to today's topic Y in this way..." They're priming the class by activating existing knowledge. You can do the same for yourself: a quick mental scan of related concepts or experiences before you start studying can prepare your brain to integrate the new information.

A well-known study strategy incorporating priming is the **SQ3R method** (Survey, Question, Read, Recite, Review). The first step "Survey" is essentially priming – you scan the chapter to get an overview. The next step "Question" has you formulate questions based on headings (again, priming curiosity). Students who use SQ3R often report feeling more focused and retaining more than if they dive straight into reading. For example, one student used SQ3R for a dense psychology textbook chapter on memory. First she *surveyed* the chapter (noticed it talked about short-term vs long-term memory, forgetting, etc.), then she *questioned* by writing down queries like "What's the difference between short-term and long-term memory?" and "What causes forgetting?" When she read the chapter fully, she was actively looking for the answers, and later she recalled the information more vividly because she remembered *seeking* it. In essence, the surveying and questioning primed her brain to receive and organize the details that came during reading.

Another illustration: A study coach on YouTube, Zain Asif, emphasizes priming as the first stage in his study methods. Before he truly studies a topic, he skims it and writes down key topics and keywords, basically giving himself a roadmap. He compares it to "laying a blueprint before building the house" – only after that does he go back and fill in the details with full study. He found that this approach drastically reduced his total study time because when he did study in depth, he rarely had to re-read or backtrack; his brain was prepared to slot each detail into a framework. His experience echoes what many top students find: spending a bit of time upfront to preview and frame a topic can make the subsequent learning phase far more efficient.

Common Misconceptions & How to Overcome Them

Some students worry, "Isn't skimming or pre-studying just extra work? What if I don't have time?" It may feel like you're studying the material multiple times (a quick pass, then a deep pass), but in practice each pass serves a different purpose and is quicker than trying to do everything in one go. Priming actually saves time overall by preventing confusion and repetitive re-reading later. To see the benefit, try it on a small scale: prime one chapter and not another, and see which one you learn faster or remember better. The difference often convinces students that priming is worth the few extra minutes.

Another misconception: "If I preview things beforehand, isn't that like cheating? Shouldn't I learn it *properly* the first time around?" This might come from a belief that struggling through cold, unprepared learning is more virtuous or that you must challenge yourself immediately. In reality, exposing yourself to an overview first isn't cheating at all – it's smart. Struggling blindly can be more discouraging than beneficial. Priming doesn't give you the answers, it just gives you context so you can learn the answers more effectively. Think of it this way: an athlete wouldn't skip the warm-up before a race – similarly, a learner shouldn't skip priming before intense study.

Chapter 6: Active Recall – The #1 Strategy for Learning Anything Faster

Scientific Explanations

If there is one technique that research consistently shows to trump others in effectiveness, it's active recall (also known as retrieval practice or the testing effect). Active recall means actively stimulating your memory during study – essentially, *testing yourself* on the material rather than just reviewing it. Why is this so powerful? When you retrieve information from your brain, you strengthen the neural pathways associated with that information. Think of memory like a muscle: every time you successfully recall something, you give that memory a workout, making it stronger and more enduring.

This is not just theory; it's been demonstrated in many experiments. Numerous studies have compared students who study by re-reading versus those who study by self-testing, and the self-testing group almost always retains more long-term. One famous study had students learn foreign language word pairs (e.g., Swahili-English pairs). One group studied the pairs multiple times; another group studied them fewer times but was tested on them more. In final recall tests, the group with more testing (active recall) remembered significantly more words than the extra-study group. Why? Because *retrieval itself is a learning event*. When you struggle to recall something, even if you don't succeed at first, the attempt primes your brain to remember it better the next time. And when you do succeed in recalling, you "re-save" that information in your memory with stronger connections (a process called reconsolidation).

Neuroscientifically, every time you recall a fact (say, "What is the capital of France?" and you retrieve "Paris"), you not only strengthen the memory of "Paris," but also strengthen the associations or cues that led you to recall it ("capital of France" -> "Paris"). Next time when you think "capital of France," the connection to "Paris" will fire faster and more surely. Also, retrieval practice often involves reconstructing knowledge (since you typically recall in your own words or steps), which engages deeper processing than recognition. Compare that to re-reading: when you read something again, you might think "I know this" because it looks familiar, but you aren't actively reconstructing it from memory, so you're not truly testing whether you can pull it out on your own.

Active recall also directly combats the forgetting curve. By retrieving information at intervals after learning, you interrupt forgetting and reset the curve each time, flattening it a bit more. It's been found that even a single recall attempt after learning can significantly increase retention compared to no recall attempt. This is why doing practice problems or quizzes a day after learning something dramatically improves how much you remember weeks later.

Another aspect: active recall helps with *transfer* and application of knowledge. When you practice pulling info from memory, you get better at using that info in flexible ways (like solving new problems or composing an essay), because you're effectively rehearsing the exam scenario – producing information without notes. Every time you simulate that while studying, you're rehearsing the actual performance you'll need later. As psychologist Henry Roediger and colleagues have noted, testing is not just an assessment tool, but a learning tool; it changes the memory, making it more recallable in the future.

Practical Applications & Techniques

Incorporating active recall into your study routine can be done in many ways, from formal practice tests to informal self-checks. Here are some methods:

- **Flashcards (Physical or Digital):** Flashcards are a classic recall tool. You have a question or prompt on one side and the answer on the back. Tools like Anki or Quizlet enable this digitally and can even schedule the cards (combining recall with spaced repetition, which we'll discuss later). The key with flashcards is to *actually recall the answer in your mind* before flipping the card. It sounds obvious, but passively looking at Q then immediately at A is not recall. You should attempt to say the answer (or write it down or visualize it) *without peeking*, then check. If you were correct, great – that retrieval attempt just strengthened that memory; if not, that's fine – now you know what to review further. A pro tip: when reviewing flashcards, don't just parrot back the exact phrasing. Try to recall the concept and maybe elaborate a bit. For example, if the card says "H_2O boiling point?", you might answer "100°C at 1 atm – that's when water turns from liquid to gas." By adding a bit of explanation, you ensure you really know it, not just the number.

- **Practice Problems and Quizzes:** For problem-solving subjects (math, physics, accounting, etc.), doing practice problems is active recall in action. Instead of just reading solved examples repeatedly, you should close the book and try to solve a new problem (or even re-solve an example from scratch without looking at the solution). Even trying to remember and write out the steps of a solution from memory is beneficial. If you get stuck, that's valuable feedback: it pinpoints exactly which step or concept is weak for you. Then you can review that specific part and attempt the problem again later. Many textbooks have end-of-chapter quizzes or problem sets – use them as intended. Also, consider creating your own questions while studying: after reading a section on, say, World War I causes, you might write down a quick quiz prompt like "List five major causes of WWI." Later, test yourself on it without notes. You can treat these as mini self-exams.

- **Active Recall Note-Taking:** Transform your note-taking process to include recall. One method is the Cornell note-taking system, which encourages a "cue" column. After class, you write questions or keywords in the margin of your notes. Later, you cover the detailed notes and use those cues to prompt your recall of the details. Another approach is after reading a section or attending a lecture, put away the source and attempt to outline the key points from memory on a blank page. Then check against your notes or textbook to see if you missed anything. By the end of your study, aim to be able to reproduce the main structure of the topic from memory. This process of writing what you remember (and checking where you forgot something) *is* active recall and highlights precisely what you need to review again.

- **Teach or Explain (without notes):** As discussed in Chapter 4 and 11, teaching is a form of active recall because you must retrieve information to explain it. Find an opportunity to explain a concept you just learned to someone else (or to an imaginary audience) *without looking at your notes*. If you can teach it clearly, you have definitely recalled and understood it. If you stumble, note those parts – that's where your memory or understanding is shaky. This method not only cements memory (since you recall and articulate it), but also highlights subtle gaps you might not notice with simple Q&A recall. Essentially, being able to *tell the story* of a concept out loud is an ultimate test of recall + comprehension.

- **Active Recall in Daily Life:** Make recall a habit integrated into your routine. For example, if you're walking between classes or on the bus, quiz yourself mentally: "What did I learn in the past hour that I can recall right now?" or "I read about Newton's laws earlier – can I recite the three laws from memory?" These casual retrieval practices keep memories fresh. Some students put sticky notes with questions on their mirror or have a friend randomly text them a question from their study material as a challenge. Be creative – the goal is to frequently challenge your brain to pull information without immediately looking at the answer, even outside formal study sessions.

- **Pre-lecture and Post-lecture Recall:** We touched on pre-testing in priming (attempting questions before learning). Similarly, after you finish studying something, do a quick *post-review recall session.* For example, close everything and try to brain-dump on paper all the key points you remember about the topic you just studied. Essentially ask yourself: "Tell me everything about [topic]" and see what you can produce from memory. Then compare to your notes to see if you missed anything. This is effectively a practice test you create for yourself immediately after learning, which helps lock in that new knowledge and shows if anything didn't stick. Even a short attempt to summarize or list main points after reading a chapter can significantly boost retention.

A compelling real-world example comes from Cal Newport's college experience (and from students he interviewed). He discovered that many straight-A students had independently figured out the power of active recall. One student described how after each class, he would create a one-page quiz for himself on the lecture content and then take that quiz later without notes. Another student would re-write major points from memory every weekend as a review. Cal himself switched from passive review to a system of "active recall files" – basically, he boiled down each class's material into a series of questions that he practiced answering without looking at his notes. The results? He found he could finish studying far earlier and still get top grades, even claiming it felt like developing a "pseudo-photographic memory" for the material by exam time. This echoes countless other success stories where students say: testing myself made all the difference.

Another example: Medical students are notorious for heavy use of active recall through flashcards (especially using Anki). A typical med student might accumulate tens of thousands of digital flashcards covering everything for their board exams. That sounds intimidating, but because these cards are reviewed daily in spaced intervals, by the time the exam comes, they have actively recalled each fact multiple times over months. Studies in medical education show that those who engage in this kind of spaced retrieval practice (through flashcards or question banks) outperform those who rely on re-reading notes or repeatedly watching lectures. In fact, a study from a medical institute emphasized that practice testing helps organize information and protects memory from interference, making it one of the highest-utility strategies. Real med student testimonials often attribute their success to doing thousands of practice questions – which is essentially active recall plus application.

A simpler everyday example: learning a language. Suppose you try to memorize vocabulary by reading a word list versus using flashcards or a recall app. The flashcard users almost always recall more words later. Additionally, techniques like trying to use the word in a sentence (without looking it up) or translating a simple story from your native language into the new language are forms of recall practice. You're forced to retrieve vocabulary and grammar rules rather than just recognizing them on a page. This leads to far better long-term language retention than passive review of lists or re-reading grammar notes.

Common Misconceptions & How to Overcome Them: A big misconception is "Testing myself is only for after I've studied a topic, to see if I know it." In truth, *testing is studying*. You don't use active recall merely as a litmus test at the end; you use it throughout the learning process to actually learn more effectively. Students sometimes hesitate to quiz themselves too early because they feel they "don't know it yet" – but that's exactly when quizzing helps the most (you will learn it by attempting to recall it). Overcome this by viewing each recall attempt, even if you get it wrong, as a learning opportunity rather than an evaluation.

Another misconception: "Active recall only helps memorization, not understanding." Actually, recall often requires understanding. For example, to answer a conceptual question from memory ("Why does X happen?"), you must grasp the concept. Also, if you realize during recall that you *can't* explain something, that prompts you to go back and seek understanding. So active recall and understanding go hand in hand. Techniques like elaborative interrogation (asking "why?" and trying to recall an explanation) directly foster understanding. In practice, students who do retrieval practice on conceptual material retain it and comprehend it better than those who passively review – likely because recall highlights what you don't understand, forcing you to address it.

A related misconception: "Active recall is tedious or time-consuming." It can feel harder than just reading notes, true – it's cognitively more demanding. But you tend to need fewer total hours of study because the time you spend yields much higher retention. If a subject normally takes you 10 hours of passive review to reach a certain level, you might reach the same level with 6 hours of active recall-focused study. Also, it doesn't always require a special setup or extra time – as shown, you can integrate quick recall exercises into your day (mental quizzes during downtime, etc.). Many find that once they incorporate recall and see the results (e.g., remembering more with less cramming), it becomes almost like a game to test themselves. The initial resistance often comes from the discomfort of facing what you don't know in the moment. Overcome that by reminding yourself that failing in practice is completely okay – in fact, desirable – because it's how you learn. Embrace the challenge aspect: it might feel tough to pull answers from your brain, but that "desirable difficulty" is exactly what makes it effective.

Chapter 7: Layered Learning – Organizing Information from Easy to Hard

Scientific Explanations

Not all learning material is of equal difficulty. Some aspects provide the foundational understanding (the "easy" broad ideas), while others add complexity or detail (the "hard" specifics). *Layered learning* is the strategy of approaching a subject in progressive layers of depth or difficulty, rather than trying to master everything at once. This method aligns with how our cognitive processing works: we build mental schemas or frameworks that we then refine and add to. Trying to absorb all details before understanding the big picture is like trying to decorate a house before the walls are up – it doesn't work well. By layering, you ensure you have a structure in mind so new info has a place to attach, which greatly enhances comprehension and memory.

Cognitively, layered learning takes advantage of *scaffolding* – a concept from educational psychology. Scaffolding means providing support and then gradually removing it as the learner becomes more competent. In this case, the initial layer (basic concepts) is the scaffold for understanding the next layer (finer details). It also respects cognitive load: learning the first layer uses some mental capacity but leaves enough free capacity to handle the next layer when you're ready. If you try to consume all layers at once, you overwhelm your working memory and end up not encoding much effectively.

Dr. Justin Sung, a learning coach, describes a "four layers of learning" model which illustrates this well. In his approach:

- **Layer 1: Logic layer** – the fundamental principles or big ideas (the foundation).

- **Layer 2: Concepts layer** – fleshing out those main ideas into coherent concepts, but still general.

- **Layer 3: Important details layer** – adding critical details that support those concepts (key examples, formulas, exceptions).

- **Layer 4: Arbitrary details layer** – memorizing the minutiae or less connected facts (dates, specific values, footnotes).

He emphasizes that starting with the logic layer is crucial; if you skip it, you end up overwhelmed by details without understanding how they fit. Conversely, once the first layers are solid, the last layer of fine details "falls into place naturally."

Research on expert vs. novice learning shows that experts see patterns and structures in information that novices don't. For example, expert chess players categorize positions by underlying strategies, not just piece-by-piece positions. Layered learning helps novices form these structures step by step. Initially, you might consciously impose a structure (like dividing a biology chapter into "overview of system, key organs, cellular mechanisms, chemical details"). With practice, you start to see these layers inherently and immediately.

Another angle: think of *desirable difficulty* again. Layered learning can introduce difficulty gradually to optimize learning. If you start too easy and never increase complexity, you stagnate; if you start at the highest complexity from the get-go, you may flounder. A layered approach ensures a ramp-up of difficulty. It's akin to level progression in a video game – each level builds on the last, providing challenge at the right time so you stay in a "flow" state (not bored, not hopelessly frustrated).

Practical Applications & Techniques

Here's how to implement layered learning in your studies:

- **Pass 1 – Big-Picture Pass:** Begin any new topic with a big-picture overview. This closely relates to priming (Chapter 5). Your goal in this first pass is to answer: *What are the main points or sections? What's the overall purpose or narrative?* Use summaries and introductions if available, or do a quick skim focusing only on the broad strokes. If it's a textbook chapter, for example, read the introduction and conclusion first, and maybe the first sentence of each paragraph to catch the drift. If it's a lecture, listen for the outline or thesis statements. At this layer, do *not* get bogged down by unfamiliar terms or details – mark them to revisit later. For instance, if you're studying the circulatory system, layer 1 might yield: "Function: transport blood; main parts: heart (pump), blood vessels (pipes), blood (fluid); big subdivisions: pulmonary vs. systemic circulation." By the end of pass 1, you should be able to summarize the topic in a few sentences or draw a simple diagram. You've basically laid down the logic or foundation.

- **Pass 2 – Conceptual Pass:** Now go deeper. Read the material fully or attend the lecture, but focus on understanding *concepts and relationships*, not on memorizing every fact. In this layer, clarify how things work and *why*. Fill in your big picture with more structure. For example, continuing with the circulatory system: now you focus on *how* the heart's four chambers pump blood, the difference between arteries and veins, the concept of blood oxygenation in the lungs vs. oxygen delivery to tissues. You might take notes under each subheading now, but still avoid excessive detail. If there's a technical detail like "the average adult has 5 liters of blood," notice it but it's not crucial yet to commit to memory. By the end of layer 2, you should be able to explain the core processes or ideas in your own words. You might still not recall exact numbers or minor exceptions, but you have a working understanding.

- **Pass 3 – Detail Pass (High-Yield Details):** Next, tackle the important details that support or elaborate on the concepts. Now is the time to memorize key definitions, formulas, dates, and names that are considered "high-yield" (i.e., likely to be tested or essential to precision). In this pass, you might create flashcards for specific facts or ensure you know precise terminology. In our circulatory example, this is where you'd memorize names like "mitral valve" or "sinoatrial node," or the sequence of blood flow through the heart chambers, or the formula for cardiac output. Because you already understand what valves and nodes *do* from pass 2, memorizing their names and functions now is much easier – they're not random terms, they're pieces of a system you grasp. As you layer in details, keep connecting them to the broader framework ("Mitral valve – oh, that's the valve between the left atrium and ventricle that I learned controls one-way flow; its name is 'mitral' which I now know").

- **Pass 4 – Review & Mastery (Fine Details, Edge Cases):** This is a polishing layer, often done via practice questions or final review sessions. Here you handle any remaining bits: rare exceptions, very specific data, tricky applications. You might not always need a formal layer 4 if layer 3 covered what you need for your purposes. But for full mastery (like in advanced study or cumulative exams), this layer ensures nothing slipped through the cracks. For example, maybe most people can skip memorizing the exact oxygen saturation percentages in arteries vs. veins, but a med student might learn that in layer 4. Or learning subtle exceptions: "All arteries carry oxygenated blood except the pulmonary artery." Because you have the context from earlier layers ("pulmonary = lung loop, so naturally that artery carries deoxygenated blood to the lungs"), noting that exception now is straightforward – it fits logically. This last layer often involves spaced repetition and lots of practice to lock in the fine points for long-term.

It's important to note that layering doesn't always mean you literally read everything multiple times fully. Often the first layer might be very quick (a skim or listening to an intro), the second layer could be the thorough reading and note-taking, the third layer might be a targeted study of the tough bits and doing practice problems, etc. The idea is the progression of depth, not necessarily four distinct read-throughs of the same text.

Practical Example of Layered Approach

Imagine preparing for an exam on World War II history using layering:

- Layer 1: Read a one-page summary of WWII or watch a short overview video. Outcome: you know the timeline and major players, e.g., "Started 1939, ended 1945; Allies vs Axis; major events like Pearl Harbor, D-Day, Hiroshima."

- Layer 2: Attend lectures or read your textbook chapters fully, focusing on understanding causes of the war, how it unfolded, and consequences. You take structured notes by theme (causes, key battles, political dynamics, outcomes). You grasp why certain events happened and how they connect, but you might not remember every date or casualty figure yet.

- Layer 3: Review notes and now start memorizing specifics: dates of major battles, names of key generals, statistics like death tolls, etc. Perhaps you create flashcards for battle dates or treaties. You also ensure you can recount specific examples (like appeasement of Hitler at Munich, or details of the Manhattan Project).

- Layer 4: Practice writing essay outlines or doing quiz questions that mix up all aspects of WWII. Address any obscure topics (maybe specific operations or lesser-known fronts) that you haven't covered. Double-check minor points. By now you have the big stuff down cold, so these finer points have a scaffold to fit into.

Connections Between Methods

Layered learning inherently incorporates priming and active recall at each stage. Priming is basically layer 1 (getting context). Active recall can be used at the end of each layer to ensure you're ready for the next: e.g., after layer 2 (concepts), you might recall the outline of the topic from memory before diving into layer 3 details. It aligns well with spaced learning too: you might do each layer on different days, which builds in spacing. It also works nicely with **organization tools** like mind maps: your first mind map might have just 1st and 2nd layer info, then you add details to it in layer 3. Essentially, layering ties together many principles – you are managing cognitive load, repeatedly reinforcing and building upon knowledge (which inherently involves recall), and structuring learning logically.

Common Misconceptions & How to Overcome Them

Misconception: "Layered learning sounds slow – will I have time to go through material multiple times?" It might seem like multiple passes are extra work, but in practice each pass is targeted and quicker than one giant all-at-once session. Layered learning often *saves* time by preventing inefficient re-reading and confusion. Also, once you get used to it, you might combine layers dynamically (sometimes you can cover layer 1 and 2 in one go because you're adept at extracting the big picture then immediately filling some details). Overcome this worry by trying it on a smaller scale: divide one chapter into two passes instead of one, and see if you learn it more solidly without extra total time.

Misconception: "Isn't layered learning just an excuse to not pay attention to details initially? What if I miss something important in early passes?" You might worry that skimming or not focusing on detail in layer 1 or 2 means you'll overlook an important point. But remember, layering doesn't mean ignoring details; it means deferring them until you have context. If something is truly important, it will show up again in your thorough read or be emphasized by your instructor – you won't miss it ultimately. The early layers are about setting up the mental framework to *hold* those details. In fact, by layer 3 you'll catch that important detail more easily because you'll see exactly why it's important. To overcome this fear, make quick margin notes when you encounter unfamiliar terms or facts in early passes (so you can come back to them). Trust the process that you *will* circle back.

Misconception: "Layered learning might make me too general – I need to know specifics!" Some subjects, like anatomy or law, have a lot of detail that needs memorizing. Layering still applies: you first learn the general anatomy (systems, organs) before memorizing every muscle name; you first learn the legal framework before memorizing particular case laws. Being "too general" initially is a stepping stone to mastering specifics. Think of it as first creating labeled bins in which to sort all the tiny items. Without the bins (categories and general understanding), your specifics will be a jumbled mess. Overcome this by realizing that being general first is not the end goal, it's the means to handle the specifics more effectively.

In summary, layered learning helps tackle complexity systematically. Start simple, then add complexity gradually. By learning in layers, you prevent overload, reinforce understanding at each step, and make the absorption of fine details much more manageable. The result is a more structured knowledge in your mind that's easier to recall and apply.

Chapter 8: Mind Mapping – The Visual Strategy for Mastering Concepts

Scientific Explanations

The human brain doesn't store information in neat linear lists; it stores information in networks of interconnected ideas (much like a web of neurons). Mind mapping taps into this by providing a visual representation of information in a network-like structure rather than line by line. A mind map starts with a central concept and branches out into related subtopics, which can further branch into details. It uses keywords, colors, and even images to trigger associations. This technique leverages several cognitive principles at once:

- **Visual Encoding:** By engaging the visual-spatial areas of the brain, we add another modality to learning. Research on dual-coding theory suggests that information encoded both verbally and visually has better recall because it has two pathways to retrieval. A mind map is essentially dual-coding your notes: the structure (layout) and often pictures or icons add a visual element to otherwise verbal information. Instead of only remembering a written paragraph, you might recall the image of your map with its distinct branches and perhaps a doodle on one branch, which helps cue the content.

- **Association and Chunking:** Mind maps literally draw connections (via lines or placement) between concepts. This mirrors how memory works by association. When you see two ideas linked on the map, you grasp their relationship instantly. Over time, recalling one node in the map helps you recall the connected node (because you trained that link in memory). Also, each branch of a mind map is effectively a chunk – a cluster of related bits grouped under a larger concept. Chunking information into groups is known to improve memory. Studies have shown that concept mapping (a similar method) can improve memory by helping students integrate new knowledge into existing frameworks, making recall cues more effective.

- **Depth of Processing:** Creating a mind map is an *active* process. You must decide what the key ideas are, how to organize them hierarchically or logically, and how to label them succinctly. This means you're processing the meaning of the material deeply (summarizing, categorizing, linking) rather than copying notes verbatim. Deep (semantic) processing aids understanding and memory – often called the "levels-of-processing" effect. In fact, one study on note-taking found that students who organized information (like in a matrix or concept map) remembered more than those who took linear notes, presumably because the former required deeper processing and reorganization of the material.

- **Engagement and Creativity:** Mind maps often encourage use of colors, drawings, and unique layouts. This not only makes the process more engaging (so you pay attention longer), but the uniqueness of your map can serve as a mnemonic device. For example, you might recall, "Oh yes, I drew a little battery icon next to 'ATP' on my mind map about cellular energy" – that visual might pop up in your mind during recall, bringing the concept with it. The brain often remembers distinctive or novel things (this is related to the Von Restorff effect), and a personalized mind map inherently contains distinctive elements that standard notes may not.

- **Whole-Brain Activation (anecdotal):** Tony Buzan, the popularizer of mind maps, claimed it engages "both left and right brain" – left (logical, linguistic) and right (creative, spatial). The left-right brain theory is somewhat oversimplified, but the point is that mind mapping is multi-faceted: it involves words, spatial arrangement, color, maybe imagery – likely creating richer memory traces than plain text.

Importantly, mind maps align perfectly with layered learning (Chapter 7). The structure of a mind map is hierarchical: main branches for layer 1-2 info, sub-branches for layer 3 details, etc. This makes complex information easier to navigate and recall, because you see the big framework and how details slot in. In fact, there's empirical evidence: a 2023 study with nursing students found that those who used mind maps had significantly better short-term and long-term recall of lecture material than those who took traditional linear notes. The mind mapping group could retrieve info more effectively even after two weeks, suggesting the technique helped in organizing core content and making it more retrievable.

Practical Applications & Techniques

Here's how to create and use mind maps effectively in your studies:

- **Start with a Central Idea:** Grab a blank sheet (often using landscape orientation works best to give horizontal space) or open a mind mapping software. Write the central topic or concept in the middle. Use a strong keyword or a simple phrase (or even a picture) that represents the subject. For example, if you're mapping a chapter on Climate Change, you might write "Climate Change" in the center and maybe draw a small Earth or a symbol like a thermometer. This central node is your map's focus.

- **Branch Out Major Themes:** From the center, draw thick branches outwards for each major section or theme of the material. Think of these as the main categories or subtopics. Each branch gets a short label – ideally a single word or a very short phrase that encapsulates that subtopic (the brevity forces you to condense the idea into a keyword). For our climate change example, main branches might be "Causes," "Effects," "Mitigation," and "Policy." Write each of these near the end of a branch radiating from the center. It helps to use different colors for different branches to give a visual separation (e.g., make the "Causes" branch green, "Effects" branch red, etc.). Making the branches slightly curved or organic-looking (instead of straight lines) can also be more visually interesting, which may aid memory.

- **Add Sub-branches for Details:** From each main branch, draw thinner branches that represent supporting details, facts, or concepts related to that subtopic. These can further branch if needed. For instance, under "Causes" of climate change, you might have sub-branches "Greenhouse Gases," "Deforestation," "Industrial Revolution timeline." Under "Greenhouse Gases" branch, you might break out further into "CO_2 – fossil fuels," "CH_4 – agriculture," etc., if those details are important. Again, keep labels concise – just enough to identify the point ("CO_2 from fossil fuels," for example). Use additional small lines or branches to connect directly related pieces. If something is a sequence, you can number the sub-branches to indicate order.

- **Use Images and Symbols:** Enhance nodes with small drawings or icons where appropriate. Even simple stick figures, arrows, or symbols can make a branch more memorable and encapsulate meaning. For emissions, you might draw a tiny factory smokestack; for "Policy" you might sketch a gavel or scales. If drawing by hand, artistry is not important – even a goofy sketch that *you* understand is fine. If using software, you can often insert icons or emoji (like a key emoji 🔑 next to a key concept, or a warning ⚠ symbol for a big risk). One med student reported remembering the cranial nerves better by drawing a mind map where each nerve had a tiny sketch of its function (like a little eye for the optic nerve). During exams, the visual memory of those sketches helped him list and recall the functions quickly. So, images can attach meaning and uniqueness to a node.

- **Emphasize Key Points with Formatting:** You can vary text size or style to signify importance. Perhaps you write extremely important terms in all caps or a larger font on your map, or put a star next to them. For example, if one cause of climate change is overwhelmingly significant (say CO_2 emissions), you might write "CO_2" in larger letters or in a bold color. Visually emphasizing key points can signal to your brain that "this one is extra important." Some people make the central idea largest, main branches slightly smaller text, sub-branches smaller yet – this gradient itself shows the hierarchy.

- **Make it Personal and Associative:** The beauty of mind maps is they reflect *your* mental associations. Feel free to add mnemonic cues or personal references. If you have to remember a list of items, you might create an acronym from the first letters and jot that near the branch. If two branches relate to each other, draw a dashed line connecting them (e.g., link "Effects" and "Policy" if certain policies mitigate certain effects). This externalizes the network of knowledge and can help with memory ("I recall drawing a dotted line from X to Y, meaning they were related somehow."). You can also dedicate a small sub-branch for "Examples" where you list concrete examples for a concept – since examples often make abstract points stickier.

- **Use During Review:** Once your mind map is made, it's a powerful review tool. Don't just admire it – use it actively. For example, cover parts of the map and test if you can recall them (active recall!). Or, even better, practice redrawing the mind map from memory on a blank sheet. This is an excellent way to see if the knowledge structure is firmly in your mind. If you can recreate the map (even a rough version) with its branches and sub-branches, chances are you know the material well. Also, before an exam, you can use the completed map as a one-page quick reference to jog your memory of how everything connects – scanning it can reactivate the whole network of info in your mind much faster than flipping through pages of notes.

- **Mind Map in Real-Time (if feasible):** With practice, some learners even take notes in mind map form during class or while reading. This can be challenging initially (because you're organizing on the fly), but it can keep you actively processing as you listen. For instance, in a lecture, you might jot the central topic at top, then as the professor moves through points, you branch them out live. However, many prefer to take linear notes in class then convert them to a mind map afterward (which itself is a great review exercise). Choose what works for you.

One student, studying European history, created a mind map for World War II. The center said "WWII (1939-1945)". Main branches were "Causes," "Major Events," "Allies," "Axis," and "Outcomes." Under "Causes," sub-branches included brief notes like "Treaty of Versailles -> German anger," "Economic Depression," "Rise of Fascism." Under "Major Events," she branched by year with key battles (each labelled, with tiny flag doodles to denote who won – e.g., a Nazi flag icon vs a Union Jack). The "Allies" branch had sub-branches for each country with leader names (and she drew a little caricature or symbol: e.g., UK – Churchill with a cigar icon, USSR – Stalin with a mustache icon). The "Axis" branch similarly had Hitler with a swastika, etc. "Outcomes" branch had sub-branches "United Nations formed," "Cold War begins," "Casualties ~60 million," etc. By creating and studying this map, she found she could narrate the entire WWII storyline in detail without flipping through pages, because her brain visualized the map and followed each branch logically. In the exam, when asked about causes, she literally saw her "Causes" branch and recalled each factor.

Another example: Some polyglots use mind maps to group vocabulary by context or themes. For instance, for learning language related to restaurants, a central node might be "Restaurant" with branches for "Ordering Phrases," "Food Items," "Customer Service Phrases," "Compliments/Complaints," each with associated target language terms and maybe little doodles (plate of food, waiter figure, etc.). Seeing words grouped by scenario can help recall them in context as opposed to a random list of 50 words. Similarly, you can mind map grammar rules (with a branch for each tense, then sub-branches for usage rules, each with an example sentence drawn in a bubble).

In sciences, mapping out complex processes (like the Krebs cycle in biochemistry) is common: you arrange the cycle in a loop on paper, each compound as a node in the cycle with arrows to the next, and side branches noting energy produced at that step. That's basically a mind map because it's not linear text – it's spatial and relational. Many students recall visual diagrams of cycles or systems far better than text descriptions; to answer a Krebs cycle question, they mentally "walk around" the map of the cycle.

Regarding evidence: beyond anecdote, as mentioned earlier, a study found nursing students who mind mapped had higher recall test scores. They reported that mind mapping helped them organize core content and retrieve it, which is exactly what many students struggle with in heavy content fields.

Connections Between Methods

Mind mapping connects with active recall in usage (you can practice redrawing from memory) and with layered learning in creation (you naturally map layers: big ideas as main branches, details as twigs). It's also a great tool for spaced review – you can gradually refine or add to your mind map across spaced study sessions. For example, first session draw major branches, later session see if you can still draw them and then add details, etc.

Priming (Chapter 5) and mind mapping can work together too: as a priming activity, you might sketch a rough mind map *before* studying to outline what you expect to learn, then fill it in after reading (this engages curiosity and prior knowledge). Also, mind mapping a new chapter after reading it is a way to force yourself to re-process and organize (deepening memory).

Common Misconceptions & How to Overcome Them

Misconception: "Mind maps look messy or childish; I prefer outlines." Some people see a colorful mind map and think it's not serious or it's chaotic. Yes, mind maps can look busy compared to a tidy outline, but that busyness reflects the brain's own rich network. If an outline works better for you, that's fine – an outline is like a text-based mind map with indentations. But many who try mind maps find they remember more because of the visual nature. Overcome skepticism by trying it on a small topic – don't worry about art or looking silly, focus on whether it helps recall.

Misconception: "Mind mapping takes too much time, I'd rather write normal notes." It's true, drawing a mind map especially with colors or images might take a bit longer than scribbling notes. But consider it part of studying; it's an active review process, not just note-taking. The time spent is offset by less time needed later to study or re-read things, because the map itself helps imprint the info. Also, with practice, you can mind map more quickly (software can help speed this up too).

Misconception: "I'm not a visual learner, so mind maps won't help me." While it's true some people think more in words than pictures, mind maps still enforce logic and connections, which benefit any learner. You can keep them mostly text if that's your style (the spatial arrangement still adds value versus linear notes). The concept of strict "visual vs auditory" learners is oversimplified – nearly everyone benefits from engaging multiple senses. So even if you're initially uncomfortable, give it a shot for a concept-dense topic and see if you recall relationships better.

In summary, mind mapping is a creative yet powerful way to study. It externalizes the network in your head onto paper, making studying more active and potentially more enjoyable. By seeing the "big picture" and details at once, and the links between them, you engage your brain in the way it likes to think. Whether you're brainstorming an essay, summarizing a chapter, or reviewing for a test, mind maps can help turn information into knowledge that's connected and easy to retrieve.

Chapter 9: Pre-Testing – Why Taking a Test Before Learning Boosts Retention

Scientific Explanations

It may sound counterintuitive: why take a test on material you haven't learned yet? You'd just get most of it wrong, right? But research shows that this "pre-testing effect" can significantly improve subsequent learning and retention. When you attempt to answer questions or solve problems *before* studying a topic, several beneficial cognitive processes occur:

- **Activating Prior Knowledge:** Pre-testing forces you to tap into whatever related knowledge you might already have, even tangentially. This is essentially priming in question form. By trying to answer, you prepare the brain for what's coming by identifying your gaps and any relevant frameworks you already know. For example, if a pre-test question asks "What is the capital of Australia?" you might think of Australian cities and realize you're not sure. Now when you study geography, that question will stand out and you'll pay special attention to info about Australia. Pre-testing thus sets up mini "quests" for your brain during learning.

- **Creating Curiosity and Readiness:** Struggling with a question generates an information gap in your mind. You become curious about the answer because you just tried and failed to retrieve it. This state of curiosity (even mild frustration) primes your brain to be more receptive to the answer when it appears, often giving you an "aha!" moment. Psychologically, when you then learn the answer, it often comes with relief or satisfaction ("Oh, I see!"), which can encode it with an emotional tag that aids memory. In essence, pre-testing makes you eager to learn what you don't know.

- **Highlighting What's Important:** If you have a pre-test before a lecture or reading, the questions often signal the key points or learning objectives. Even if you get them wrong, you now know what you should be focusing on when you do study. For instance, if a pre-test asks about a concept you've never heard of, you'll be on the lookout for that concept during the lecture. It functions similarly to an advance organizer: it gives structure to the upcoming material by pointing out likely main ideas.

- **Engaging Retrieval Processes Early:** Attempting retrieval (even unsuccessfully) has been found to enhance later memory for that item. In one study, participants who tried to recall word pairs and failed, then studied them, retained more than participants who just studied without a pre-try. This suggests that the act of trying to retrieve primes the memory such that when the correct information is learned, the brain "binds" the new information to that prior attempt. It's like creating a question-shaped slot in your mind; when you later find the answer, it snaps into place firmly. Essentially, pre-testing leverages retrieval practice benefits *before* learning, so that the eventual learning is more robust.

- **Error-Based Learning:** Pre-tests lead to making errors (and that's fine!). Research by Kornell, Hays, and Bjork (2009) showed that making wrong guesses (with later feedback) resulted in better retention than just reading the correct answer from the start. The hypothesis is that errors, when corrected, produce a strong memory trace because the correct information gets contrasted with the wrong attempt, clarifying the concept's boundaries. Also, being aware of your misconception makes you pay extra attention to the correction. This ties into "feedback-driven metacognition" – you become acutely aware of what you misunderstood and you focus on the correction.

In essence, pre-testing is a combination of desirable difficulty and priming. It makes initial learning a bit more effortful (because you're challenged up front), but that extra effort leads to deeper processing and memory formation. It also somewhat replicates test conditions early, reducing test anxiety and building familiarity with how questions might be phrased. It's like practicing the skill of retrieving/applying knowledge, not just the knowledge itself.

Practical Applications & Techniques

Here are ways to incorporate pre-testing into your study routine:

- **Do Practice Questions First:** If you have access to a question bank, review problems, or study guide questions for a chapter, try answering a few *before* you thoroughly study the chapter. Don't worry that you might not know much – either make your best guess or even write "I have no idea." For example, before reading a chapter on photosynthesis, attempt the end-of-chapter questions. This will help you identify what parts of the material are likely important and which terms or concepts you need to pay special attention to. Then, after studying, come back and do those questions again to see improvement (which is satisfying and reinforces learning).

- **Pre-read Questions in Texts:** Many textbooks have questions at the end of sections or little "Think about it" prompts in the margins. Read those questions *before* you read the text section. Try to predict an answer or at least consider what knowledge would be needed. Then, as you read, you'll naturally find those answers. Similarly, if a textbook states objectives like "After reading this, you should be able to explain X," use those as pre-test queries: ask yourself if you can explain X now (likely not) but keep that question in mind. This primes you to latch onto the explanation of X when it appears.

- **Use Study Guides or Past Exams:** If your course provides a study guide or you have access to past exam questions, don't save them all for the final review – employ them early. For instance, before a related lecture, glance at relevant past exam questions. Even try outlining answers based on what you *think* you know from prior knowledge. You'll probably be incomplete or off-track, but when that topic is covered in lecture, your brain will connect it to that question. Essentially you create a mental placeholder ("So that's what they were getting at in that question!").

- **KWL Technique:** A classic approach in education is the KWL chart – What I *Know*, What I *Want* to know, and (later) What I *Learned*. Before learning a topic, list what you already know (activates prior knowledge) and then list questions you want to be answered or things you wonder about (this is a form of generating your own pre-test questions). Essentially, you're setting up a personal test: "I want to know these 5 things." Then you learn, and afterward, you answer them. Framing learning as answering questions is very effective. So, for each new chapter or topic, maybe write down a series of questions (often, headings can be turned into questions). That list of questions becomes your pre-test: try to answer from prior knowledge (likely you can't fully), then study and see if you can answer them properly.

- **Brainstorm or Solve from Intuition:** In problem-solving domains, before learning a formula or method, try solving a simple instance with intuition or prior knowledge. For example, before learning a new math formula, see if you can derive or guess how to solve a sample problem. Even if you fail or only get partially correct, you might come up with a plausible but slightly wrong approach. When you learn the formal method, you can contrast it with your approach and see why the formula works better, which deepens understanding. Another approach: look at a complex worked example, cover the solution, and attempt to figure it out conceptually. After struggling, reveal the solution and compare – this will highlight steps you didn't think of or misconceptions. Essentially, you're pre-testing yourself on problem-solving steps and letting mistakes guide your focus.

- **Quizzes at the Start of Study Sessions:** If you're studying solo, you can start each study session with a quick self-quiz on the topic you're about to review. For instance, if you plan to read Chapter 5 on DNA replication, begin by writing down 3–5 questions you suspect are key (even if you aren't sure of the answers). Or if you have an interactive tool/website that generates quiz questions, use it upfront (some digital textbooks have pre-chapter quizzes). Some exam-prep books even have "pre-assessments" – do those first rather than skipping to the reading.

- **Embrace Mistakes:** When pre-testing, adopt a mindset that getting things wrong is expected and actually helpful. Don't let wrong answers discourage you; instead get curious: "Aha, I didn't know that – can't wait to find out." Always follow up by finding out the right answer or explanation when you study, otherwise the benefit is lost. It's the correction of the mistake that really sticks. If you try pre-testing but then never fill in the gaps, that's just leaving holes. So, ensure you check your answers later and actively learn the correct information.

- **Mini Pre-tests in Lectures or Groups:** If you're in a study group, you can incorporate pre-testing with each other. For example, before discussing the reading, ask each other a few questions like "What do you think concept X means?" or "How would we solve this kind of problem?" Then after everyone confesses ignorance or gives it a shot, go through the material together and revisit those questions. In class, teachers often do this with polls or pre-lecture quizzes (and there's a reason—they see improved learning). As a learner, you can simulate that environment yourself by challenging yourself or peers with pre-questions.

There's an interesting study where one group of students was given a pre-test (with no expectation they'd know much) on a set of material, then everyone studied the material, and another group just studied without pre-test. On the final test, the pre-tested group outperformed the others significantly. Qualitatively, students often express surprise that trying (and failing) at questions first helped. But when asked later, they remembered those specific questions and their correct answers well—often because they remembered what they answered wrong and the "aha" when they learned the right answer. This anecdote underscores the pre-testing effect: struggling first made the learning more memorable.

Think of the game show *Jeopardy!*: Contestants are given answers and must respond with questions, so they practice by exposing themselves to vast trivia and trying to recall under pressure. In a way, that's constant testing even on unknown facts. Similarly, you can treat your learning like a quiz show game – looking for answers to interesting questions – rather than rote reading. That mindset can make studying more engaging and effective.

A student preparing for the MCAT (medical college admission test) might use a question bank of thousands of questions throughout their months of study, often doing questions on a topic before fully reviewing it. They find that guessing and then reading explanations makes them remember the material better than if they had just read a textbook chapter passively. It guides their studying (they learn what they specifically didn't know) and it keeps them more alert when they do go review because they're thinking, "Oh, so that's how this is applied."

Connections Between Methods

Pre-testing is closely tied to active recall (Chapter 6) – it's basically a type of recall attempt, just timed before learning rather than after. It also complements priming (Chapter 5) – it primes not only with context but with questions that need answering, focusing your attention. It's a desirable difficulty at the outset (like layering but starting with a challenge). It obviously relies on feedback to be useful (you must eventually check answers, which ties to error correction ideas). Combined with spacing, you might pre-test, learn, then test again later – an optimal cycle for memory.

Common Misconceptions & How to Overcome Them

The primary misconception is "What's the point of testing if I haven't learned it? It'll just discourage me or be a waste of time." The point is not to score well – it's to *prime* and *prepare* your brain. Remind yourself that the pre-test is not an evaluation of you; it's a learning strategy. It's actually fine (even expected) to get a 0% on a pre-quiz. If you're worried about discouragement, use it as a game: "Let me guess, and see how close I get – no harm done if I'm wrong." Then enjoy the improvement you see afterward.

Another misconception: "Pre-testing wastes time I could spend learning." Actually, the initial time is small (a few questions perhaps), and it makes your later study more efficient (you focus on the right things, you possibly need fewer read-throughs because you have a mission to find answers). The net effect can be saving time. To convince yourself, experiment: for one chapter do no pre-test and see how long/hard it is to study and recall later; for a similar chapter, do a quick pre-quiz first and see if studying feels more pointed and sticks better. Often the difference is noticeable.

In summary, pre-testing takes advantage of our brain's love of questions and challenges. By flipping the typical order (test after study) and testing first, you ironically end up learning better. So next time you crack open a chapter or start a new unit, throw yourself some questions or attempt a problem cold turkey. You stand to gain a lot in how well you encode and later retrieve that knowledge.

Part 3: Advanced Study Tactics for Mastery

Having covered core strategies in Part 2, we now move on to Part 3, which dives into advanced tactics that further refine your approach to learning. These chapters will focus on optimizing how you capture information (effective note-taking), how you use teaching as a tool to learn, how to mix different topics (interleaving) to boost mastery, how to lock knowledge into long-term memory (spaced repetition), and how to prepare efficiently for high-stakes tests by tying everything together.

In Part 3, we'll build on the principles from earlier chapters. Keep in mind how techniques like pre-testing, active recall, priming, layering, and mind mapping can continue to play a role as we discuss these advanced methods. The goal is to fine-tune your study strategy so that you're not just learning effectively but also integrating and applying all these techniques to achieve mastery in any subject.

Chapter 10: The 3-Step Process for Effective Notetaking (Recall Question Method)

Scientific Explanations

Many students take copious notes, yet later find those notes unhelpful or cumbersome when studying. Effective note-taking is not about transcribing everything – it's about processing information, organizing it, and turning your notes into learning tools (especially for active recall). An efficient note-taking system not only records information but also sets you up for reviewing and self-testing later on.

One proven approach divides note-taking and review into three steps: **Capture**, **Question/Condense**, and **Review/Recall**. Breaking the note-taking process into these stages aligns with cognitive science principles like spaced repetition and active recall. Let's outline the 3-step process and the reasoning behind each stage:

1. **Capture:** This first step happens during the lecture or reading. Your goal is to capture key information and ideas – essentially externalizing what you don't want to trust to memory in the short term. However, "capture" doesn't mean write every word. Research on laptop note-taking versus hand-written notes has shown that verbatim note-takers (often on laptops) tend to remember less than those who can't write everything and thus have to synthesize. The ideal capturing method therefore focuses on key terms, definitions, and concise points, using abbreviations

and symbols to speed up. Structuring the notes during capture (with headings, bullet points, indentation, etc.) provides organization which will help later. Leaving margins or spacing for later annotations is also important (this ties into the next step). Essentially, the capture phase is about *encoding* the information in an external form efficiently. It's fine if these notes are a bit incomplete – they will be fleshed out in step 2.

2. **Question/Condense:** This crucial second step is often done shortly after note-taking (within a day is optimal). Here you transform your raw notes into a format optimized for active recall. In the popular Cornell note-taking system, this is where you fill in the "cue" column with questions or keywords. The idea is to create recall prompts for each segment of your notes. Doing this soon after the lecture ensures the material is still fresh enough that you can articulate good questions or summaries, but also after a bit of a gap so you're recalling from earlier in the day (leveraging a small spacing effect). By condensing notes into questions or brief summaries, you are engaging in *elaboration* and *reorganization* – both deepen understanding (levels-of-processing effect). You're also implementing generation effect (coming up with questions is self-generation of content, which improves memory for that content). This step essentially turns passive notes into an active study tool.

3. **Review/Recall:** Now, and in subsequent study sessions, you use the questions or cues to test your

memory of the material periodically (spaced practice). Cover the notes, look at the question prompts, and attempt to recall the answers or explanations. This is classic retrieval practice. Studies like Karpicke & Roediger (2008) have shown that practicing retrieval (even without additional study) can double long-term retention compared to re-reading. Scheduling multiple quick reviews – e.g., later that day, the next day, later that week, etc. – yields the benefit of spaced repetition, flattening the forgetting curve. Because you've made questions, doing these recall sessions is straightforward (less friction than if you had to decide what to test yourself on each time). The results of step 3 feed back: if you consistently miss a question, you know to review that content more or perhaps clarify your notes or ask for help.

This 3-step method addresses common pitfalls: Students often take notes and then never revisit them (no recall practice), or they try to re-read everything (inefficient and often passive). By incorporating a systematic recall component, notes become living documents that one interacts with multiple times, not just archives.

Practical Applications & Techniques

Let's break down how to apply the 3-Step Process concretely:

- **Step 1: Capture (During Class or Reading)** – Write down main points, key facts, and any explanations or examples you deem necessary. But write smartly:

o Focus on key terms and definitions. Don't try to capture full sentences if a shorthand will do. Use symbols ($\rightarrow$ for leads to, $\uparrow$ for increase, Δ for change, etc.) to speed note-taking. For instance, if the teacher says "Photosynthesis produces glucose and oxygen," you might jot "Photosyn: CO_2 + H_2O $\rightarrow$ glucose + O_2 (in chloroplast)." This shorthand conveys the essence without full sentences.

o Structure matters: use headings or bullets to group related points. If the lecture has sections, clearly label them in your notes (underline or highlight when a new topic starts). This will help when you form questions later – you'll naturally group questions by section.

o Leave a margin on the left side (if using Cornell method) or space between major points where you can later write cues/questions.

o If you miss something, mark it (e.g., "??" or a blank line) so you know to fill it in afterward (maybe ask a classmate or check the textbook).

o If a question pops into your head during class, scribble it in the margin with a "?" – the instructor might answer it later, then you can fill it in; if not, you've generated a question to investigate (this flows nicely into step 2 as well).

- **Step 2: Question/Condense (Soon After)** – Within 24 hours (so the material is still reasonably fresh), process your notes:

  o Formulate recall questions in the margin or on flashcards based on your notes. For example, if your notes say: "Osmosis = diffusion of water across semipermeable membrane from low solute conc to high solute conc," form a question like "What is osmosis?" or even better, "How does osmosis work?" If you have a list in your notes (e.g., 3 causes of French Revolution), frame a question: "List three major causes of the French Revolution."

  o For processes or sequences, create fill-in-the-blank or how/why questions. E.g., notes: "In mitosis, chromosomes line up at equator during metaphase," question: "During which phase of mitosis do chromosomes line up in the middle?" This forces you to recall a specific detail of the process. Essentially, turn notes into Q&A form.

  o Condense facts into bite-sized answers. If an answer would be very long, break it into multiple questions. This is important – overly broad questions like "Explain everything about concept X" are not as useful as specific ones that target single ideas. Aim for each question to be something that can be answered in a few sentences or a short list. This modular approach also helps you identify specifically where your memory fails if you can't answer one.

o Write a brief summary at the end of your notes or at the end of each section. A few sentences that capture the essence – think of it as answering "In sum, what was this section about?" This summary itself can serve as the answer to an overarching question like "Summarize the mechanism of ____ in your own words."

o Ensure clarity in your notes now: if any shorthand was ambiguous or you left blanks, fill them by checking the textbook or asking someone. This is the time to tidy up misunderstandings while the lecture is fresh.

o The result of Step 2: your page of notes now has a column of questions or cue words on the left (or you have a parallel set of flashcards/questions prepared). The main body of detailed notes is on the right (or on the back of flashcards). You've basically prepared a self-quiz out of your notes.

- **Step 3: Review/Recall (Afterwards, Repeatedly)** – Now use those questions to test yourself over time:

  o Cover your detailed notes (or flip flashcards to the question side), and attempt to answer each question from memory. This is like having a built-in flashcard system if you used the Cornell style margin questions.

o   If using physical notes, you might recite the answer, then uncover to check. If using flashcards or a digital app, you know the drill: see question, think answer, then reveal the answer and grade yourself.

o   Schedule quick, frequent reviews: For example, each evening, quickly run through the questions from that day's classes. End of week, do a bigger review of all questions from that week. Because your questions are succinct, running through them doesn't take as long as re-reading all notes. You can just attempt an answer for each – if it's solid, move on; if not, mark it to revisit.

o   Periodically (especially before exams), do a more thorough recall session: try to brain dump an entire topic using your question list as prompts – e.g., write out or speak out everything you know about each question without looking at notes, then check for any missing pieces.

o   Use summaries for big picture refresh: recall your summary sentences without looking, to ensure you still grasp the overall concept before diving into details.

o   Update your notes if needed: During these recall sessions, if you realize something is unclear or you discovered new info (maybe from homework or further reading), add a note or refine a question. Your notes/questions set is a living document that can evolve.

A Concrete Example of the 3-Step Method: Suppose you're taking a biology class:

- During class on the heart (Step 1, Capture): you write notes like:

  o "Heart anatomy: 4 chambers (2 atria, 2 ventricles)."

  o "Valves: AV valves (tricuspid, mitral), Semilunar valves (pulmonary, aortic) – prevent backflow."

  o "Blood flow: body → RA → RV → lungs → LA → LV → body."

  o "Cardiac cycle phases: diastole (filling), systole (pumping)."

  o "Conduction: SA node (pacemaker) → AV node → Bundle His → Purkinje fibers." (You mark "SA node" with a star because you know that might be important but the detail was quick.)

- After class (Step 2, Question/Condense): you generate questions like:

  o "Name the four chambers of the heart."

  o "What is the function of the heart valves?"

- o "Describe the path of blood flow through the heart (starting from body)."

- o "What are the main phases of the cardiac cycle and what happens in each?"

- o "Outline the electrical conduction pathway of the heart." For each, you think through the answer and maybe jot short hints as needed. You clarify: "SA node – where impulse starts (pacemaker)" as an annotation on the conduction line.

- Later that day and week (Step 3, Review/Recall): You cover the answers and quiz yourself:

  - o Q: Four chambers? You recall "right atrium, right ventricle, left atrium, left ventricle" – correct, check notes to verify phrasing.

  - o Q: Function of valves? You answer "prevent backflow of blood; the AV valves separate atria and ventricles, semilunar separate ventricles from arteries." Check notes – yes, matches what you have.

  - o Q: Path of blood flow? You recite "Body → RA → RV → Lungs → LA → LV → Body." Spot on.

  - o Q: Phases of cardiac cycle? You recall diastole vs systole definitions – good.

  - o Q: Conduction pathway? You struggle a bit: "SA node → AV node → something... Purkinje?" You check – you forgot "Bundle of His." Now you know you need to remember that element, so you might highlight or make a mnemonic (maybe "Sally And Harry Picked Berries" = SA, AV, His, Purkinje, just as a silly aid).

- ○ Next review, you focus on that one and get it right.

Many top students credit active note-taking methods for their success. For example, Cal Newport (author and straight-A student) often mentions in interviews a method he used: he took detailed notes in class (Capture), then that same day condensed each lecture's notes into a one-page summary or list of questions (Question/Condense), then he would study by covering answers and practicing recall (Review/Recall). His results were a 4.0 GPA with less stress – he finished studying far before exams because his system meant he was learning consistently, not cramming. He essentially created a giant list of quiz questions (active recall files) which he would systematically go through. This method closely mirrors our 3-step approach.

Another learning YouTuber, Zain Asif, promotes what he calls the "Recall Question Method." It essentially says: after learning a small chunk (say a few pages), write a question for it and later quiz yourself with those questions. He emphasizes doing it in realistic conditions (like using blank paper, not peeking) and claims it ensures "you never have to restudy again" because your recall practice cements the info long-term. Students who tried it report they no longer need to re-read notes multiple times because converting notes into Q&A format means they learn them in one or two passes thoroughly.

The Cornell note-taking system, developed in the 1950s by Walter Pauk, has been studied: one experiment had students take Cornell notes (which involves cues and summary) versus just copying notes, and those who used Cornell and actually utilized the cues and summary in study scored higher on tests. Because they had essentially built a self-quizzing mechanism, they engaged in retrieval practice instead of passive review.

Another anecdote: A law student dealing with large volumes of case law information took notes on cases, then in step 2 wrote questions like "In [CaseName], what rule was established?" and "What were key facts leading to [Decision]?" When prepping for finals, she quizzed herself on those. She realized she was practicing retrieving legal rules and applying them as answers – exactly the skill needed for writing exam essays. So, her note-taking strategy directly translated to exam performance.

Connections Between Methods

This 3-step note process inherently uses active recall (step 3). It naturally builds in spacing because you review notes after class (short interval) and then again later. It fits with layered learning – your notes themselves reflect layers (main ideas as headings, details indented), and summarizing after class reinforces the conceptual layer while forming questions preps the detail layer for review. It's priming too: good notes can prime advanced learning; also, making questions before reading a text is like pre-testing (some students preview a chapter by turning headings into questions, which is a merge of priming and pre-testing). And one can incorporate mind maps in step 2 if they prefer – some might convert linear notes into a mind map (organizing and condensing visually) then recall from that.

Common Misconceptions & Overcoming Them

Misconception: "Taking and reworking notes takes too much time; I'd rather spend that time reading or doing problems." While it does take extra time to process notes after class, it's high-value time. It reduces the time needed later by ensuring you learned it right the first time. It's like sharpening the saw – a bit of time invested that pays off in efficiency. Students who just read or do problems without consolidating notes often end up re-reading multiple times because it didn't stick. Try it on one topic and see if you end up studying that topic less later because you nailed it early.

Another: "My notes are fine as is; I can just re-read them." Re-reading notes is passive; turning them into questions forces active engagement. If your notes feel "fine," test that by seeing if you can answer questions about them a day later without looking. If not, that shows the need for the question/recall strategy. The step 2 might reveal that some parts of your notes weren't clearly understood (because you struggle to form a question or summary) – better to realize that sooner than during the exam.

One more: "I'm too busy to review notes after class." It doesn't have to be long – even 10 minutes per class to jot cues and summary can make a huge difference. Perhaps integrate it into your routine (right after class before you leave campus, or in the evening as a quick homework). Once you see improved test results or less pre-exam panic, it will justify the time.

In summary, note-taking isn't just about writing things down – it's about setting up the stage for remembering and understanding them later. By capturing information efficiently, then actively transforming notes into questions and using those questions for recall practice, you turn your note-taking from a passive record into an active learning process. This approach ensures that by the time you get to the exam, you've already been testing yourself all along – so the exam is just another (albeit final) recall session, not an unfamiliar challenge.

Chapter 11: Teaching as Learning – The Power of Explaining Concepts to Others

Scientific Explanations

They say the best way to learn something is to teach it. This isn't just a proverb; there's science behind it. Known as the *protégé effect* or "learning-by-teaching," studies have found that when learners expect to teach material to someone else, they learn it more effectively and organize it better in their minds. When you teach or explain a concept (to an actual person or even just out loud to yourself), several beneficial things happen:

- **Active Recall and Elaboration:** Teaching forces you to retrieve information from memory and explain it in your own words – which is active recall – and to elaborate on it, connecting ideas and forming analogies so someone else can understand. According to research (e.g., Nestojko et al. 2014), students who expected to teach recalled more key points and structured their recall more coherently than those who expected to just be tested. That's because in preparing to teach, you naturally impose structure and highlight what's important (so you can stress it to the learner) and link concepts logically to explain them clearly. In doing so, you deepen your own understanding and memory of the material.

- **Exposure of Gaps (Metacognitive Benefit):** When you try to teach, any area you don't fully understand becomes quickly evident – you might stumble, or your "student" might ask a question you can't answer, or you realize you skipped a step in the explanation. This immediate feedback (even if it's just noticing your own confusion) tells you where your knowledge is shaky so you can target that area. It's much better to discover these gaps in a practice teaching session than in a high-stakes setting like an exam or real-world application. Essentially, teaching acts like an active self-test of how well you *truly* know the material.

- **Improved Memory Encoding:** Explaining out loud engages more senses and cognitive processes than silent studying. You hear yourself speak (auditory input), you might use gestures or draw diagrams while explaining (kinesthetic and visual input), and you're processing ideas verbally. This multimodal engagement likely creates more and stronger memory traces. Additionally, by teaching, you often turn the information into a narrative or logical flow ("first this happens, which leads to that, therefore...") – and our brains remember stories and logical progressions better than disjointed facts.

- **Confidence and Motivation:** As you successfully teach and clarify concepts, you build confidence in your mastery of the material. This confidence can reduce anxiety in test or application situations ("I taught this to my friend, so I can handle it on the test"). Also, knowing that you will teach someone can motivate you to learn more diligently – you don't want to teach incorrectly, so you prepare thoroughly.

Studies have found that just the expectation of having to teach made students adopt more effective study strategies spontaneously (they summarize more, seek main points, etc.).

- **Relational and Big-Picture Thinking:** Good teaching requires focusing on the relationships between ideas and building a coherent picture. So, when you teach, you constantly relate new information to prior knowledge ("this is similar to that concept we learned last week" or "here's how these two ideas interact"). Doing this helps you form a more integrated understanding. You move beyond memorizing facts to seeing the framework or system because you have to explain that framework to someone else.

One phenomenon observed is that sometimes learners, while explaining something, will fill in a gap by reasoning it out on the spot (similar to Feynman's technique of trying to explain and noticing gaps). Teaching not only reveals gaps but can also *help* you bridge them as you attempt to answer a student's question or clarify a point (learning while teaching).

Practical Applications & Techniques

You don't need to be a formal teacher to use teaching as a learning tool. Here are ways to harness this effect:

- **Teach an Imaginary Class or Rubber Duck:** It might feel silly, but explaining a concept out loud as if to a novice – even if no one is actually there – can be very effective. For example, after studying a chapter, stand and pretend you're giving a mini lecture on it. Or explain it to a "rubber duck" (an object or pet) on your desk. This technique is famous in programming: explaining your code to a rubber duck often helps find bugs. Similarly, explaining a concept to an inanimate listener forces clarity. If you get stuck, that's a red flag about what to review. You can even anticipate simple questions ("why does that happen?") and ensure you answer them. Because an imaginary student won't judge, this is a low-pressure way to practice.

- **Study Groups & Peer Teaching:** In a study group, divvy up topics and have each person teach a portion to the others. For example, for a set of readings, each member becomes the "expert" on one reading and explains it to the group. The act of preparing to teach that reading ensures the "teacher" learns it deeply, and the others benefit from their explanation. Encourage the listeners to ask questions; if the peer teacher can answer, great – if not, it identifies something to collectively clarify. Research suggests even expecting such a teach-back improves how the student initially learned the material. If you don't have a study group, you can simulate one by agreeing with a classmate to take turns teaching each other parts of the syllabus.

- **Feynman Technique (Teach a Child):** Richard Feynman famously used a method where he'd try to explain a complex concept in the simplest terms (as if teaching a child). The steps: study a concept, then write or speak an explanation for a layperson (or child). Use simple language. Whenever you struggle or use jargon, note that as a gap, go back to the source to understand better, then simplify and continue. Repeat until you have a clear, simple explanation. This technique forces you to truly understand the content well enough to break it down, which means you will not forget it easily. You can apply this by literally writing a one-page "explain to a newbie" summary of what you learned and checking it against your notes for completeness and accuracy.

- **Tutor Someone Else:** If possible, tutor a friend or a younger student in a subject you've learned. For example, if you did well in calculus, help someone taking it after you. Tutoring not only reinforces your foundational knowledge but often the student's questions or mistakes will teach you something new or reveal assumptions you didn't realize you had. Many graduate students report that teaching undergrads made them truly master their undergraduate content. So even informal tutoring can solidify core knowledge and sometimes show edge cases you hadn't considered. Plus, explaining concepts to different people forces you to adapt and deepen your explanations.

- **Teach in Writing (Blogs, Forum Responses):** Writing is another form of teaching – you have to clarify your thoughts in order to explain them coherently. For example, after mastering a tricky economics concept, you might write a blog post titled "In simple terms: What is inflation?" Writing it out for a general audience means you must get it right and clear. You can also answer questions on forums like Stack Exchange: find a question someone asked that you know about and try writing a helpful answer. People might ask follow-ups or give feedback. Many have found that blogging or explaining concepts publicly not only helps others but cements their own knowledge (and sometimes highlights subtle points they double-check while writing).

- **Pretend to be the Teacher on an Exam:** This is a mental trick while studying: create potential exam questions and answer them, effectively role-playing both teacher and student. By making questions, you approach the material like a teacher thinking "How would I test this? What's a good question that covers this idea?" This perspective helps you identify the core learning points and see if you can stump yourself. Then answering your own question is essentially teaching yourself the solution. So, you're designing a mini quiz (teaching role) and solving it (student role). It's an active way to engage with content beyond what's given to you.

- **Use Visual Aids While Teaching:** When explaining, use tools like drawing a diagram on a whiteboard or piece of paper. This not only aids the explanation for your "student," but the act of creating a visual (mind map, flowchart, etc.) reinforces the connections in your own mind. And the ability to produce a diagram from memory is a sign of mastery – if you can draw it while teaching, you definitely know it. Incorporate elements from earlier strategies: e.g., "Let me draw a quick mind map on the board to show how these concepts connect" – doing so requires recall + organizing in real-time.

- **Be Mindful of the "Illusion of Teaching":** Sometimes one might think "I explained it; therefore I understand it completely," when maybe there were minor errors or oversimplifications that a novice wouldn't catch. After teaching (especially if it was to someone who may not know if you were right or wrong), do a self-check: verify from reliable sources that your explanation was accurate and you didn't accidentally propagate any errors. This ensures teaching others doesn't entrench a misunderstanding. That said, usually teaching will highlight uncertainties for you, but this step guards against false confidence from teaching incorrectly.

One famous demonstration of the learning-by-teaching effect: in an experiment, one group of students was told they would have to teach the material to other students after learning it, and another group was told they'd be tested on it. In reality, all were tested. The "teach" group not only remembered more but also had better organized recall and answered more conceptual questions correctly. Observers noted that these students approached studying differently – they tried to understand thoroughly and articulate the logic, almost mentally preparing how they'd explain it. That mindset shift improved their learning outcomes.

Anecdotally, a medical student found a study group in which they routinely "teach-back" to each other to be invaluable. Each member regularly presented mini-lectures on topics to the others. He realized when he first had to teach topics, he'd sometimes find mid-explanation that he didn't know the "why" behind a step – which then drove him back to clarify it later. By exam time, he felt much more prepared, and they all performed well. He credited the teach-back sessions with revealing their blind spots long before exam day.

Another common scenario: Many students find that when they study by themselves, they *think* they know something until they try to explain it to a friend or family member and suddenly find themselves stuck. For example, you might feel you understand a physics concept, but when you attempt to explain the principle to your roommate, you realize you can't quite articulate it clearly or you can't answer a basic follow-up question. This experience is a sign that you need to deepen your understanding – and because you attempted to teach, now you know exactly what to focus on. After you clarify it, you'll likely never forget that moment and the correct reasoning.

Even informal acts like telling your parent what you learned today in class can have this effect: it forces you to recap and explain, which ironically helps *you* solidify it (and your parent might ask a naive question that actually is illuminating, who knows!).

Connections Between Methods

Teaching is like an ultimate integration of many study strategies:

- It involves active recall (you have to remember content to teach it).

- It encourages elaboration and making connections (you naturally relate ideas to give someone the big picture).

- It creates desirable difficulties (explaining can be hard, but that difficulty pays off).

- It's effectively spaced practice if you teach after learning and maybe again in review sessions.

- It can even incorporate pre-testing: a student's question might pre-test you on something you hadn't thought of.

- It pairs well with Feynman technique (which is essentially teaching on paper to yourself).

- In note-taking, some people imagine while taking notes, "How would I teach this?" and structure notes accordingly (like headings as if they were slide titles).

- If you used mind maps or outlines, teaching someone forces you to simplify and present that structure clearly, which is basically using those tools actively.

Common Misconceptions & Overcoming Them

"I'm not an expert; I'll just end up teaching wrong info." It's true you need to be careful – you shouldn't spread misinformation. But teaching as a study strategy doesn't mean you go open a class; it can mean teaching back to your study group or a friend who knows you're practicing. To avoid reinforcing wrong info, always review your sources afterward to ensure your explanation was correct (as noted above). And if your friend asks something you can't answer, admit "I'm not sure – let's look it up." That process is itself valuable learning. Over time, as your confidence builds, you will be teaching correctly because you'll have caught and fixed earlier mistakes. And the fear of embarrassment can actually motivate you to double-check facts beforehand, which means you learn them better.

Another misconception: "Teaching others takes extra time I could use studying." However, teaching *is* studying – one of the most effective forms. If you spend 30 minutes explaining concepts to your peer, that 30 minutes is not lost; it's arguably equivalent to hours of passive reviewing. Many find that tutoring or study groups take time but they end up needing less time alone to master the material. If you truly have no one to teach, teach yourself by writing or speaking to an imaginary audience – it still works.

Finally: "I'm not good at explaining; I'll just confuse myself." Like any skill, you get better with practice. Start by explaining small chunks to yourself. The first few times might feel awkward, but you'll quickly notice improvement. And you will definitely notice how much clearer *your* understanding gets. It's okay if your first attempts are clunky – you're not giving a TED talk, you're just learning by doing. Over time, you'll become more concise and structured in explaining, which will reflect in how clearly the knowledge is organized in your mind.

In summary, teaching others (or pretending to) is a powerful method to test and improve your understanding. It combines retrieval practice, elaboration, and reflection. By explaining concepts in simple terms and answering questions about them, you reinforce your knowledge and identify exactly where you need to focus more. So don't wait to be a professor – start "teaching" as a student and reap the learning benefits.

Chapter 12: Interleaving – How Mixing Subjects Boosts Learning

Scientific Explanations

Traditional studying often involves "blocking" – focusing on one subject or one type of problem for a long period before moving to the next (e.g., do all math problems from chapter 1, then all from chapter 2, etc.). *Interleaving* is the practice of alternating between different topics or problem types within a single study session, rather than blocking them. While blocking can produce a sense of fluency (because you get into a groove on one type of problem), research shows that interleaved practice leads to better long-term retention and better ability to distinguish between concepts or choose the correct method when needed.

Why does interleaving work?

- **Forces Retrieval and Discrimination:** When different problems or topics are mixed, your brain cannot rely on the context of doing the same thing repeatedly – you have to actively figure out what kind of problem each one is and recall the appropriate approach from scratch. This is crucial because in real tests or real life, problems come in mixed forms and you must identify what principle to apply. Interleaving trains you to notice differences and similarities between problems, thus improving your ability to choose the right formula or concept at the right time. A classic study by Rohrer & Taylor (2010) on learning math formulas found that students who practiced with interleaved problem sets (varied shapes intermixed) scored much higher on a later test than those who did blocked practice (one shape's problems then next). The interleaved group learned to identify which formula to use by recognizing problem patterns, whereas the blocked group got good at one formula at a time but got confused when all types were mixed later.

- **Desirable Difficulty:** Interleaving makes practice more challenging in the short term (since you have to reset your brain for each new type of problem or topic). This is a *desirable difficulty* – something that feels harder initially but yields greater benefits for memory and transfer. Because you can't go on autopilot, you engage more deeply each time you switch. It also slows you down a bit and initial performance might be worse than with blocking, but that extra effort leads to stronger encoding and versatility.

- **Prevents Contextual Dependency:** If you do 20 of the same type of problem in a row, you may become good at executing the procedure while you're in that context, but you might actually be learning *the pattern of the practice*, not truly how to apply the method independently. (For example, if you do 20 derivative problems in math, by the latter ones you're just applying the same steps without thinking if it's a derivative problem or an integral problem – your brain knows by context they're all derivatives). Later, when confronted with a single problem in a different context, you might not recognize it requires those steps. Interleaving ensures you practice retrieval of knowledge in varying contexts – making it more adaptable. It's akin to training in different environments to be ready for anything.

- **Greater Engagement:** Mixing things up can reduce boredom and mental fatigue. The novelty of switching tasks re-engages your attention. There's evidence that attention tends to wane with repetitive tasks, so alternating between tasks can keep your brain alert, which can indirectly enhance learning. (Although this isn't exactly multitasking; it's sequential, not simultaneous task switching.)

- **Cross-Topic Connections:** Sometimes interleaving subjects leads to insights or connections that you might not notice if studied separately (though this is more incidental). For example, you might interleave physics and math problems and realize a certain mathematical method applies nicely to a physics situation, something you might have missed if you studied each in isolation.

Interleaving is especially studied and effective in domains like mathematics, where students must learn to choose among different formulas or methods, and in motor learning (like sports) where practicing a mix of skills yields better retention and transfer. But it can apply to any scenario where you have multiple skills or topics that could otherwise interfere or be confused if not practiced in discriminative fashion.

Practical Applications & Techniques

How can you apply interleaving in studying?

- **Mix Problem Sets:** If you have homework or practice problems in different categories, don't do them grouped by category, but shuffle them. For example, instead of doing all algebra problems then all geometry, alternate them: do an algebra problem, then a geometry one, then maybe back to algebra, etc. One approach is to create a mixed set of problems from various sections. If your textbook lists problems by section, select a few from each and do them in alternating order. If need be, use a randomizer (roll a die, use a random number generator) to pick which problem to do next, forcing variety. The key is that when you pick up a new problem, you should not automatically know which solution technique it requires – you should first have to think "What kind of problem is this? Which concept does it belong to?" That thought process is part of learning.

- **Alternate Subjects During a Study Session:** Say you plan a 2-hour evening study block and you need to cover two subjects (Chemistry and History). Resist doing 1 hour of Chem followed by 1 hour of History every time. Instead, try shorter intervals: e.g., 30 minutes Chemistry, then 30 minutes History, then back to 30 min of Chemistry, then 30 min of History. This is interleaving at a subject level. It may feel a bit jarring the first few switches, but you'll adapt. Ensure each segment is long enough that you get something done (5 minutes is too short; 20-30 minutes is a good chunk). This approach also inherently spaces your review of each subject (because you return to Chem after a break with

History in between, etc.). It keeps your mind fresher – after focusing hard on Chemistry for half an hour, switching to History can feel like a small mental break because it uses different skills, and vice versa, rather than 60 minutes in one where the latter half you might zone out.

- **Subject Rotation in Weekly Schedule:** On a larger time scale, design your weekly study schedule to rotate topics more frequently. For instance, instead of dedicating all Monday to Biology and all Tuesday to Chemistry, do a bit of both each day or alternate within the same day. Many courses purposely space topics (you don't learn all of one topic in week 1 and all of another in week 2 – they mix them across weeks) because revisiting subjects after gaps improves retention. You can simulate that even if your course doesn't: e.g., Monday morning: Bio, Monday afternoon: Chem, Tuesday: Bio then Chem again, etc. This way you inherently intermix and space practice. Research (like Cepeda et al.'s studies on spacing) indicates memory benefits when you revisit a subject after working on something else.

- **Flashcard Shuffling:** If you use flashcards for things like vocabulary or facts, always shuffle the deck. Don't study cards in the same order every time or grouped by chapter (unless you're specifically doing it the first time). A good flashcard program will mix them automatically. For example, if learning historical dates, mix different periods so you have to recall which era an event belongs to, not just memorize it in the order of the textbook chronology.

If learning languages, mix themes (don't study all "food" words together and then "clothing" words; shuffle them so you practice recall without context clues).

- **Practice Different Problem Types Together:** In mathematics or subjects with subtopics, after you have learned say three types of problems, instead of practicing each type separately, do a practice session where problems of all three types are mixed randomly. For example, if one chapter covers volumes of spheres, cylinders, and cones, don't do all sphere problems then all cylinder, etc. Mix them: that way, for each problem, you must decide which formula to use based on the shape, training you to pay attention to what distinguishes a sphere problem from a cylinder problem. This dramatically improves ability to solve new problems because in a test you first need to identify the problem type.

- **Simulate Test Conditions:** Every so often, do a self-made mock exam that covers everything in a mixed way, as real exams typically do. This is essentially interleaving entire topics. It not only tests your knowledge under exam-like conditions (time pressure, no notes), it also ensures you can fluidly jump from e.g. a chemistry question to a physics question to a math question if it's a comprehensive exam. You can compile a set of questions from past quizzes or assignments across different topics and attempt them in random order.

- **Caveats (Micro-Interleaving):** Interleaving is most beneficial when you have related topics that could be confused or where choosing the right approach is part of the skill. If subjects are completely unrelated (like Spanish vocab and Organic Chem problems), interleaving them might not produce the same discrimination benefit (though it still spaces them and can keep you energized). So, use interleaving particularly within a subject or within a skill category. For entirely unrelated tasks, the benefit might simply be variety (which helps mood/attention, but not necessarily memory for content cross-domain). Tailor interleaving to where it counts: mix similar-but-different things to train your brain to tell them apart.

- **Interleave within a Single Subject Session:** Even if focusing on one class's material, you can interleave types of tasks. For example, if studying history, instead of reading one long chapter then doing all review questions, you might read a section, then try a question on it, then read the next section, then attempt a question on the previous combined with current, etc. For skills: if doing language study, instead of separate blocks for speaking, listening, reading, writing, you can cycle among them in one session to keep them all sharp.

A study on batting practice in baseball found that players who faced a mixed sequence of pitches in practice (fastball, curve, slider, random) performed better in games than those who practiced hitting, say, 15 fastballs then 15 curves then 15 sliders. The interleaved group had to *recognize* the pitch type each time (improving that cognitive skill) and couldn't just get into a timing groove for one pitch, which mirrored real game conditions where you never know what pitch is coming. Similarly, students who did interleaved math sets (e.g., geometry formulas for different shapes intermixed) outperformed those who did blocked sets on later tests (as mentioned, Rohrer's study). They often reported it felt harder or more confusing during practice, yet their test scores were higher.

Another example: a student studying for AP exams had AP Calculus and AP Physics. Many physics problems required calculus, but not all. By mixing calculus practice with physics problems in her study sessions, she got much better at quickly seeing how to apply calculus in physics contexts and not confusing, say, when to use which formula from either domain. She noted that doing one then the other in big blocks earlier hadn't given her as much insight as mixing them where she sometimes had to think, "Am I dealing with a physics principle here or just a pure math problem disguised in words?"

Even for subjects like foreign language learning, some interleaving can help: switching between practicing grammar exercises and vocabulary usage in sentences can keep you from getting complacent in one or the other. Or mixing listening exercises with speaking drills in one session – it forces your brain to adapt and stay engaged, somewhat similar to cross-training in athletics to build all-around ability.

Connections Between Methods

Interleaving ties closely with spacing – mixing subjects inherently means you are spacing them out instead of doing one in a massed block. It also enhances retrieval practice by forcing you to recall method or knowledge at each switch rather than having it fresh from doing a nearly identical problem just before. It can connect with teaching or Feynman technique; for instance, you might interleave explaining a concept with solving a problem.

One must be careful not to confuse interleaving with multitasking: interleaving is *serial* – you do one thing then another, not simultaneously. It's more about sequencing practice than doing two things at once (multitasking can degrade performance, whereas interleaving improves long-term performance after initial difficulty).

Interleaving can incorporate pre-testing or self-quizzing – for example, mixing up questions from different chapters is both interleaving and a form of retrieval practice. In note-taking, instead of studying one section of notes in isolation, you could intermix questions from various sections which is again both spacing and interleaving of content.

Common Misconceptions & Overcoming Them

Misconception: "Interleaving will just confuse me, especially if topics are similar." It's true it might feel confusing at first because you're not getting that "block" comfort of context. But that confusion is actually where the learning happens – you learn to resolve it by telling the topics apart. Think of learning music: practicing scales vs practicing a piece with varied passages. If at first intermixing problems confuses you, step back and ensure you really understand each topic individually, then gradually mix. Also, interleaving doesn't mean random chaos every minute; it can be a moderate mix that still gives your brain some footing with each switch.

Another: "Switching tasks means I won't get deeply into any of them." Actually, as long as you give each a fair amount of time, you'll still reach depth; you just won't go into a semi-automatic mode. Some fear it's like not focusing. However, think of how a teacher structures a class: rarely one monotonic activity for a whole hour, they often change things up to keep students engaged and cover multiple examples. Interleaving is a bit like self-teaching that way. The key is to keep segments long enough to complete a thought. If you find you switch too fast, you can adjust (maybe 15 minutes was too quick, try 30).

Finally: "It's more fun to finish all of one type then move on." Sure, it can be satisfying to check off "done chapter 1 problems." Interleaving might feel like leaving things incomplete longer. One way around this psychologically is to define a mixed set as the goal: e.g., "I will finish this problem set that contains a mix from chapters 1-3" – then you still get the completion satisfaction when the whole set is done, plus you interleaved within it. Over time, when you see better results or find studying less dull, you might naturally prefer mixing up tasks.

In summary, interleaving introduces a constructive level of difficulty by shuffling practice. It trains your brain to be agile in recognizing problems and applying knowledge, which pays dividends in test situations and real-world scenarios where things aren't neatly labeled or sequenced. While it might challenge you more during studying, it's one of those counterintuitive techniques that yields stronger mastery and adaptability.

Chapter 13: Spaced Repetition – The Formula for Long-Term Knowledge Retention

Scientific Explanations

One of the most robust findings in cognitive psychology is the *spacing effect*: we remember information better when our learning is spread out over time, rather than crammed in a single session. Spaced repetition takes advantage of this by reviewing material at strategically increasing intervals. Each time you revisit the information after some delay, it interrupts the forgetting process and strengthens the memory trace. With each spaced review, the rate of forgetting slows (because the memory becomes more solid), meaning you can wait longer for the next review.

The mechanics:

- When you first learn something, you might start forgetting it within hours or days. If you review it just as you're about to forget (when recall has gotten a bit effortful but before it's lost), you essentially *boost* the memory back up. Ebbinghaus found that each additional review stretches the forgetting curve further out – implying you retain it longer each time.

- Each time you successfully recall or relearn, the memory reconsolidates in the brain – often adding more contextual cues or neural connections (e.g., you recall it in a different place or mood, adding new associations). This makes the memory more retrievable in diverse situations. Also, spacing usually involves sleeping between sessions, and sleep helps consolidation (so spacing by days with sleep cycles is ideal).

- Spaced repetition is essentially repeated retrieval practice spaced out. We know from retrieval practice research that the more you successfully retrieve, the better you remember. *Spacing* those retrievals out (versus massing them) means you practice retrieving when it's harder, which yields a greater long-term benefit (this is that desirable difficulty concept again – retrieving after forgetting some is more beneficial than retrieving right away).

- It's also an efficient use of time: spacing means you don't keep reviewing what's already fresh in short-term memory; you review when it's in danger of being forgotten. Studies by Cepeda et al. (2006) found that properly spaced review schedules can dramatically reduce the number of study sessions needed to achieve a given level of recall, compared to non-spaced or overly massed study. Essentially, spaced repetition gives you more "bang per review" than cramming or reviewing too soon.

On a neural level, repeated stimulation of certain memory pathways over time fosters *long-term potentiation* (LTP) – strengthening synapses. If that stimulation happens all at once (cramming), some LTP occurs but it decays if not revisited. If it's reinforced periodically, the synapses get repeated reinforcement at crucial times, likely leading to structural changes (like growth of new synaptic connections) that underlie more permanent memory storage (involving gene expression and protein synthesis in neurons – processes that take time and are aided by rest).

In practice, spaced repetition often involves reviewing content right before you would have forgotten it. For example, you might recall 90% after one day, 70% after a week – so reviewing around that one-week point is good, then maybe next in 3 weeks, then maybe 2 months, etc. Algorithms (like in flashcard software) can help predict these optimal intervals, or you can do it manually by planning out review sessions.

Practical Applications & Techniques

To apply spaced repetition:

- **Use Spaced Repetition Software (SRS):** Tools like Anki, SuperMemo, or Quizlet's long-term learning mode implement spacing algorithms. You input flashcards or Q&A, and each day the software gives you cards due for review. When you answer, you grade how easy or hard it was; the software then schedules the next review sooner if it was hard or you forgot, and later if it was easy (because it's strong and can wait longer). Over time, intervals expand to days, weeks, months, even years. For example, a new card might show up 1 day later, then 3 days, then 7 days, then 21 days, then 2 months, 6 months, 2 years, etc., as long as you keep remembering it. This ensures you don't waste time reviewing something too frequently or neglect something until it's completely gone.

- o Many students have had success learning languages, medical facts, exam prep content using Anki. It offloads the task of scheduling reviews to an algorithm – you just have to do whatever comes up in your daily queue.

- **Leitner System (manual spacing):** If you prefer physical flashcards, the Leitner box system is a simple manual way to space reviews. Set up, say, 5 boxes. Box 1 = review daily, Box 2 = every 2 days, Box 3 = weekly, Box 4 = biweekly, Box 5 = monthly (you can adjust intervals). Start all new flashcards in Box 1. Each day, test yourself on Box 1's cards. If you get one right, promote it to Box 2; if wrong, keep it in Box 1 (or demote it if it was in a higher box). Then each session, also review any cards in Box 2 that are scheduled (like if it's the correct day for Box 2), promoting or demoting as needed, and so on for Box 3 etc. Over time, cards you know well move to Box 5 (very infrequent review) and cards you struggle with stay in lower boxes (more repetition). This is spacing in action, calibrated by your performance.

- **Schedule Reviews in Calendar:** If you study by topics without flashcards, plan to revisit each topic after certain intervals. For instance, after initially learning a chapter, schedule a quick review 1-2 days later (just a glance at notes or self-quiz), another one about a week later, then another 2-3 weeks later. Keep a study journal or use reminders to prompt you. On those review sessions, actively recall key points or redo one or two problems (no need to re-read entirely if you can recall well). If it's solid, you might schedule one more check in a month or two; if you struggled, schedule a sooner review. Think of it like "watering a plant periodically, not drowning it all at once." You give the memory a chance to fade slightly, then refresh it, each time making it more drought-resistant.

- **Spaced Reading:** If you're reading dense material like textbook chapters, instead of one marathon session per chapter, break it up: read half the chapter, then take a break or read something else (space out); later or the next day, *recall* what you read in a brief summary, then continue reading. Also, plan to re-read summaries or notes after a few days. This fosters spacing in reading comprehension. Another tip: do multiple short reading sessions separated by time, rather than one long reading of multiple chapters – you'll recall more because your brain had spacing between sessions to consolidate each portion.

- **Cumulative Review:** Make part of your weekly routine a short review of past material in a spaced way. Example: each Sunday, do a 30-minute "look back" at progressively older topics: last week's (brief review), last month's (maybe list what you remember first, then check notes for gaps), last term's (if relevant, just a quick quiz or memory jog). This ensures nothing is completely lost if it's something you need long-term. If the course is cumulative, this is essential because fundamentals from early on should stay fresh throughout.

- **Use Spare Moments:** Spaced repetition works well in short bursts, which fits into downtime. For example, use a flashcard app while commuting or waiting in line – those small windows of 5-10 minutes across days add up and are perfect for spaced review. Instead of one 2-hour block of flashcards, doing 15 minutes each day for 8 days yields better retention and is easier to fit in. Many find it's less mentally taxing too – a little each day beats a huge session once a week.

- **Integrate with Note-taking:** As in Chapter 10, if your notes are question-based (Recall Question Method), spaced repetition can simply be going back to older notes' questions after some time and seeing if you still can answer them. Mark those you forget and try again sooner. Essentially treat your note questions like flashcards in an SRS manner: quiz yourself on past chapters periodically, not just before the exam.

- **Don't Neglect to Increase Intervals:** Some folks review too often because they're anxious to forget nothing. But if you review too soon (when you still remember most of it well), it's less efficient. If something was easy to recall after 1 day, push the next review further out (maybe a week or more) and use that freed time to focus on items you did forget or to learn new material. Over-reviewing can lead to plateau – trust the forgetting curve: allow a bit of forgetting to set in, then refresh. It's more potent. The first gap might be short (1 day) but then let it grow.

- **Remember Sleep and Health:** Spacing inherently involves leaving time gaps, and often that includes sleep, which is beneficial for memory. Ensure those intervals include restful nights; research suggests memory traces consolidate during sleep, especially when learning is spaced across nights. Also, physical exercise in between sessions is shown to help memory (possibly by boosting brain-derived neurotrophic factor, etc.) and at least creates separation between study sessions to enforce spacing.

Hermann Ebbinghaus himself used spaced repetition to memorize nonsense syllables efficiently after discovering how quickly they fade. In modern times, spaced repetition software like Anki has a massive following among language learners and medical students. For instance, many med students credit Anki with helping them memorize thousands of facts for board exams. They input their lecture facts into Anki, which then paces their reviews. They might review a card after 1 day, 3 days, 7 days, 14, 1 month, 3 months, etc. They find that by exam time, even if they haven't looked at a fact in a month or two, they still recall it, thanks to the prior spaced reviews that gradually built retention.

A famous anecdote: Piotr Wozniak, the creator of SuperMemo (one of the first spaced repetition algorithms), used spaced repetition to memorize massive amounts of information and optimized his entire life around it – his recall abilities are extraordinary, though his lifestyle is extreme. But the principle has been proven by countless studies: a meta-analysis by Cepeda (2006) looked at hundreds of experiments and concluded spaced practice is far superior to massed practice for long-term retention (with optimal intervals depending on how long you need to remember – e.g., to remember something for 1 year, you might want spaced reviews up to a few months apart).

Another example: polyglot Gabriel Wyner (author of *Fluent Forever*) emphasizes using spaced repetition for vocabulary and grammar to move them to long-term memory, so he can recall them even years later. He might learn 30 new words in one day but then relies on an SRS to review those words tomorrow, 4 days later, 10 days later, etc. That way, when speaking months down the line, those words are readily available, whereas if he crammed them all in one day and never revisited, they'd largely be gone.

Connections Between Methods

Spaced repetition is basically the scheduling backbone that can incorporate active recall (Chapter 6) – you do retrieval at each spaced interval; interleaving (Chapter 12) – because if you have a stack of cards from various topics, it inherently mixes them; and priming – initial short revisit might prime for deeper second learning session. It's essentially layering over time: each recall may allow you to add a deeper layer of understanding or connection because you see it in a new context.

It complements any study technique: no matter how you study (reading, notes, flashcards), doing it in spaced sessions beats one long cram. It's particularly potent when combined with retrieval practice (like flashcards or self-quizzing) as opposed to spaced re-reading (which still helps, but not as much as spaced testing). If you use Cornell notes, scheduling when to cover your notes and test yourself (as we advised in Chapter 10 to do later that day, next week, etc.) is spaced repetition by design.

Common Misconceptions & Overcoming Them

Misconception: "If I space too much, I'll forget nearly everything and waste time relearning." If you space too widely, yes, you might need to spend time relearning some parts. The trick is to find that sweet spot where recall is effortful but not lost. Modern algorithms are quite good at this. If doing manually, err on slightly shorter intervals at first until you gauge your retention. Also not everything must be perfectly timed – even somewhat spaced (like reviewing weekly vs daily) yields benefits.

Another: "Spacing feels inefficient because I have to re-study what I partially forgot." It can feel that way, but that re-study when you partially forgot is exactly when learning strengthens. It's like muscle growth – you have to let the muscle rest (and slightly atrophy) then work it again. Yes, you re-encounter info, but each time at a deeper level. Trust that it's more efficient long-term than one and done. Over time, the amount you forget between sessions becomes less, so it stabilizes.

Some feel: "I don't have the discipline to keep a schedule; I'll probably just cram before tests." Using tools or building habits can help. SRS apps send daily reminders. Putting small daily review sessions in your calendar and treating them like brushing your teeth (just a daily routine) can integrate spacing. Once you experience going into an exam needing only a light review because you've been doing spaced work, you might not want to go back to cramming stress.

Spacing may not give the immediate satisfaction of feeling "done" with a topic, since you constantly revisit it. But the payoff is when you realize at the end of the term you remember earlier chapters better than students who moved on and forgot.

In summary, spaced repetition is about timing your learning optimally. By revisiting material after your brain has had time to rest (and almost forget), you challenge your memory and reinforce it much more than continuous study. It's a cornerstone of effective long-term learning. While it requires planning and consistency, tools and habits can make it manageable. If you incorporate spacing, you'll find that cumulative exams, future courses building on prior knowledge, or professional recall of facts are all much easier to handle – what you learn truly stays with you.

Chapter 14: Efficient Test Preparation – How to Retain Information Without Cramming

Scientific Explanations

Many students equate "test prep" with "cramming," i.e., stuffing knowledge into short-term memory right before an exam. While cramming can lead to a short-lived performance boost, it usually fails to create durable memory (information often fades quickly after the test). Moreover, cramming often means massed practice, which, as we've seen, is inferior to spaced practice. Efficient test preparation uses the strategies we've discussed – spacing, active recall, etc. – to ensure you retain information long enough and can apply it under exam conditions, all without the stress and burnout of last-minute panic.

Key principles for efficient test prep:

- **Plan Backwards (Spacing Out Reviews):** By knowing the test date, you can plan multiple review sessions leading up to it. This leverages spaced repetition (Chapter 13) instead of a single massive review. For instance, if a test is in 3 weeks, schedule perhaps 3 cumulative reviews of the content, each spaced several days apart (like end of week 1, end of week 2, and two days before the test). Research by Anderson & Schunn suggests that spaced-out self-testing over weeks drastically improves final exam performance compared to a single cram session. Also, by planning backwards, you reduce overload right before the test – you'll enter exam week with most topics already refreshed previously.

- **Active Recall and Practice Testing:** Instead of re-reading notes or re-watching lectures as primary study, efficient test prep heavily uses practice tests or active recall of potential questions. It's basically doing what you'll do on the test (retrieving info, solving problems) repeatedly beforehand. This strengthens memory and reveals gaps. Studies (like Karpicke & Roediger 2008) show that students who spent time self-testing retained about 50% more a week later than those who spent the same time re-studying, even if they initially got tested items wrong. So, quizzes, flashcards, or even writing out essay outlines from memory are "gold" for test prep.

- **Simulate Exam Conditions:** Practicing under exam-like constraints (timed, closed book, writing full answers) can improve performance. It's partly psychological – you become familiar with the pressure and format, reducing anxiety – and partly cognitive: you train retrieval fluency under those conditions. Also, simulation helps you calibrate how to manage time and which strategy to use when (connected to interleaving; a mixed practice test simulation covers everything).

- **Focus on Weak Areas (but don't ignore strengths):** Efficient prep means diagnosing which topics you're weak in (perhaps via a pre-test or noticing recall difficulty) and allocating more effort there, while still intermittently practicing strong topics to maintain them (spacing). This targeted approach is more productive than blanket reading of all notes. It's supported by metacognitive research – high performers actively monitor and address their weaknesses, rather than just re-reading everything equally.

- **Elaboration and Organization in Review:** When reviewing, it's helpful not just to memorize but also to connect and categorize. Summarize entire units in your own words, create concept maps of how ideas relate, teach key points to an imaginary audience (Chapter 11 technique) – these methods deepen understanding, which helps memory and application. A student who can see connections between chapters can apply knowledge more flexibly (good for complex test questions) and is less likely to forget isolated facts (because they're linked in a network).

- **Preventing Overload (Spacing Out Study Time):** The brain can only encode so much at once. Marathon cramming sessions lead to diminishing returns as attention and cognitive resources deplete (cognitive overload as discussed in Chapter 3). For retention, it's more effective to have shorter, distributed sessions with breaks. Research on work/rest cycles (like Pomodoro technique usage) shows better focus and retention over time. Also, sleeping between study sessions is critical: pulling an all-nighter impairs memory consolidation – evidence indicates that a sleep-deprived brain retains new info far less effectively. So efficient test prep includes good sleep and maybe a final review the evening before, then rest – rather than an all-night cram which ironically might cause underperformance and forgetting soon after.

- **Emotional and Contextual Cues:** When you study in a state similar to test state (alert, maybe a bit of pressure via timed quizzes), you also exploit state-dependent learning – you're training yourself to recall under slight stress, making it easier to do so during the real stress. Also maintain confidence: spaced practice and seeing progress in recall ("I could recall this from last week!") boosts confidence, which reduces exam anxiety. Lower anxiety can improve recall (since extreme anxiety can block retrieval). Efficient prep thus isn't just about knowledge, it's about building confidence through proof of competence (via practice tests).

Practical Applications & Techniques

Putting this into action:

- **Make a Study Schedule:** Break down the material and assign specific days for review of each chunk, leaving the final 2-3 days for comprehensive practice. For example, if you have 6 chapters and 3 weeks until test: week1 - review ch1-2 (with practice questions), week2 - review ch3-4, week3 early - review ch5-6, and final days do practice exam or mixed questions covering all chapters. Buffer some catch-up time in case some chapters take longer. Stick to the schedule as much as possible; adjusting is okay but avoid compressing everything to the end. This backward planning ensures spaced reviews and prevents last-minute overload.

- **Use Active Recall Tools:** As we've hammered on, incorporate flashcards or self-quizzing regularly into your prep. Perhaps every study session starts with a quick quiz on previously studied topics (spaced recall warm-up), then you study new stuff, then ends with a quiz on what you just studied. That ensures things are actively processed and eventually moved to spaced rotation. If your course provides question banks or if you have a textbook with questions, use them extensively rather than rereading. Aim for retrieval and application, not just recognition.

- **Create a "Cheat Sheet" (for studying only!):** Synthesize the entire course on one or two sheets – key formulas, dates, concepts, with minimal hints. The act of making this is a review (you decide what's crucial), and having it allows quick refreshes. After making it, test yourself to see if you can recall what's on it without looking. If allowed, practicing making a summary sheet trains you to condense info quickly – but the main use is you have a go-to for quick last-minute checks on details, freeing your brain to focus on understanding and applying rather than holding every detail in working memory.

- **Practice Under Timed Conditions:** A week or a few days before the exam, do at least one timed session where you answer questions or write an essay exactly as if it's the exam. This will highlight if you have issues with time management or if under pressure you blank on something you thought you knew (which indicates maybe you need more practice on that or a better memory trigger). It also gives insight: maybe you spend too long on certain problem types – then you can plan an approach (like "if I don't solve in 5 min, I'll move on and come back later").

- **Simulate Testing Environment:** Especially if the test is on computer or in a specific format, practice that way. If open-ended, practice writing full answers; if multiple-choice, practice eliminating options. Also, if you can, study at least once in the same room or same type of room as the exam (context-dependent memory can help – though it's a subtle effect, familiarity might ease nerves; but it's secondary to the cognitive benefits). Essentially, don't always study in perfect comfy conditions – occasionally replicate exam-like conditions (quiet, sitting upright at a desk, etc.) to acclimate.

- **Use Past Exams or Create Predicted Questions:** Past exams or sample questions are gold. Try solving them without notes, then check with notes or solutions. For subjects without clear question banks (like literature essay), practice outlines for possible prompts, maybe get feedback from peers or instructors if you can. If past exams aren't available, try to guess potential questions (which is easier if you engaged in pre-testing in learning). This speculation exercise itself is beneficial – it forces you to think from the examiner's perspective (which often aligns with highlighting what's important).

- **Cumulative Frequent Reviews vs One Big Review:** Instead of one huge study session right before, do cumulative mini-reviews frequently (like weekly quizzes throughout the term). By test time, you've basically been studying all along. Then your final pre-exam review is just another spaced review (maybe with focus on toughest bits). Some classes have built-in cumulative quizzes; if not, self-impose them. It saves you from the dreaded scenario of trying to relearn 3 months of material in 2 days.

- **Take Care of Logistics:** Efficient prep also means reducing extraneous stress. So, double-check exam logistics: time, venue, allowed materials (so you can practice with allowed formula sheets or calculators). If you know you get anxious, incorporate relaxation techniques in prep (like a short meditation after studying to associate calm with the material). Knowing you've systematically prepared often is the best antidote to anxiety.

Consider two students preparing for the same exam:

- Student A doesn't study much until the weekend before. Then he spends 12 hours on Saturday and 12 hours on Sunday reading notes, highlighting, maybe redoing some homework, but mostly massed reviewing. He is exhausted, and by exam time on Monday, he recalls maybe just enough but is mentally fried; two weeks later, that knowledge is largely gone. Also, during the exam he struggled to recall an early-chapter formula because he had only skimmed it Sunday amidst everything else.

- Student B started studying 3 weeks out. She studied 2 hours every other day: reviewing two chapters at a time with flashcards and doing practice problems. She also took a practice exam one week before, which showed she had trouble with Chapter 5 problems. She then spent extra time on Chapter 5 and asked her teacher to clarify one concept. The night before the exam, she reviewed her concise cheat sheet and did a few flashcards, then got a good sleep. On exam day, she felt relatively calm because everything felt like *déjà vu* (she had basically done similar questions in practice). She aced the test and weeks later, she could still recall key concepts because of all the spaced retrieval. This scenario demonstrates how planned, spaced, active studying outperforms panic cramming in both performance and retention.

Another example: many professional exams (like the MCAT, LSAT, etc.) practically demand long-term prep. Successful candidates often plan months ahead with scheduled practice tests and iterative review. They avoid cramming by sticking to a study plan where the last week is just light review because the heavy lifting was done systematically earlier. They often mention feeling confident going in because they'd simulated test conditions and knew what to expect.

Connections Between Methods

This chapter essentially emphasizes using all previous methods in concert for test prep:

- **Spacing (Chapter 13):** central to avoid cramming.

- **Active Recall (Chapter 6) and Pre-testing (Chapter 9):** practice tests and flashcards simulate retrieval and show where you stand.

- **Interleaving (Chapter 12):** a typical exam covers mixed topics, so practicing in mixed sets (like doing a cumulative practice exam) directly helps.

- **Teaching (Chapter 11):** a lot of students find that explaining confusing concepts to a peer in study sessions nails it down for them come exam time. Teaching each other in a study group is effectively a review method addressing weak points.

- **Note-taking and Mind Mapping (Ch10 & Ch8):** By test time, you hopefully have excellent notes or mind maps. Efficient prep uses those as tools: e.g., you might redraw a mind map from memory as a review (covering active recall of all related points), or you quiz yourself from your Cornell note questions. If you've been doing that all along, test prep is just continuing the same practices. Good notes also make creating a cheat sheet or summary easier, as you've distilled info already.

- **Layered learning (Chapter 7):** In test review, you might re-layer: first refresh broad ideas (perhaps by writing an outline of each chapter from memory to ensure you remember high-level), then review important details that you might forget, rather than trying to re-memorize every trivial detail. Use the outline to navigate what's crucial.

- Also overcoming misconceptions: test prep is often where illusions of competence (Chapter 4) are shattered or confirmed. Frequent self-testing prevents that by making sure by exam time you truly know your stuff, not just think you do because you re-read.

Common Misconceptions & How to Overcome Them

Misconception: "I do well when I cram, why change?" Some students manage decent grades by cramming, leading them to think it works. But consider long-term retention (a year later, do you recall it?) and stress levels. Also, as material accumulates in advanced courses, cramming might hit limits (you can't cram an entire textbook overnight). If you're content with just short-term recall, maybe cramming "works," but if you aim for genuine mastery or need to build on knowledge (like sequential courses or career skills), cramming short-changes you. And one day, if multiple exams cluster, you can't physically cram for all simultaneously. So, adopt better habits early. Try prepping for a smaller test with spacing and see if you perform better with less stress; that personal evidence can motivate change.

Misconception: "I don't have time to do spaced study, I barely finish homework as is." It might seem like adding extra reviews is extra time, but spaced study can coincide with homework (if you treat homework as practice and space it out instead of doing it last minute). It's also about efficiency: if you learn it right initially and reinforce it quickly, you might save time by not re-learning. Perhaps restructure a bit: instead of two hours on one subject at once, try one hour today, one hour tomorrow (that's spacing without spending more total time). Or combine methods: use flashcards during mundane activities to sneak in spacing. It often doesn't require huge extra time, just re-allocation of existing study time. Also, consider that many homework sets or classes purposely include periodic quizzes or cumulative sections – use those as built-in spaced opportunities. If truly swamped, at least do mini spaced reviews (even 5-10 minutes recall sessions here and there). Something is better than nothing.

Misconception: "Finals week is inherently cramming; there's no other way." True, finals week is busy. But efficient test prep means prepping *before* finals week. If you wait until finals to start studying the term's material, you'll cram by necessity. Instead, treat every week as prepping for finals in small doses (like the cumulative review idea). Then during finals, you're mostly doing final polishing and lots of practice, not first-time serious study. Many top students start reviewing for finals 3-4 weeks out in small increments. By finals week, they might just do targeted problem sets and rest well. If you have multiple finals, rotate subjects each day (interleaving + spacing!). Also, integrate exam prep earlier: e.g., some do a mid-term self-made "midterm" even if class doesn't have one, to prepare better.

Misconception: "Right before the exam I must study everything or I'll feel unprepared." This is anxiety-driven. If you've spaced your learning, trust your preparation. A brief last review (especially morning of, if exam is later) can warm up recall, but avoid trying to *relearn* anything new on the last day. It's better to focus on mental readiness (sleep, slight review to activate memory, gather any needed supplies). If you find you always feel the need to re-read everything pre-exam, it suggests you don't trust your memory – improve that by practicing recall in the lead-up so you *know* you know it. Then you can use pre-exam time to just glance at your summary sheet or solve one simple example to get in the mindset, rather than frantically flipping through pages.

In summary, efficient test prep is about studying smarter, not harder – applying the science-backed techniques to reduce total study time and stress, while enhancing performance and retention. It's the culmination of everything learned in this book: you apply priming (looking at content ahead of time), active encoding (taking good notes), layering knowledge, actively recalling, connecting ideas via mapping, teaching where possible, interleaving practice, spacing it out, and doing targeted review. The result is walking into the exam confident, well-rested, and ready – without sacrificing health or sanity. And an added bonus: what you learn for the test will stay with you long after, forming a solid foundation for future learning or professional use, rather than evaporating like crammed facts often do.

Conclusion: The Future of Learning & Mastering Any Subject

Over the course of this book, we've journeyed through the science of effective learning – uncovering why the old habits of cramming, passive review, and information overload fail us, and replacing them with powerful, evidence-based strategies. By now, several key themes should stand out:

Active engagement is crucial – whether through recalling information, visual mapping, or teaching others, it's the effortful retrieval and processing that cements knowledge. **Spacing and layering** our study combats forgetting and builds durable memory structures. And **making connections** – between ideas (through mind maps and analogies) or between study sessions (through spaced repetition and interleaving) – transforms isolated facts into integrated understanding.

Perhaps the most profound takeaway is that *learning how to learn* is a game-changer. No longer does studying have to mean drudgery or uncertain results. You now have a framework: prime your brain before diving in; organize new information in layers; record it actively in visual or question form; solidify it by recalling and applying it in varied ways; reinforce it over time with strategic review. This framework doesn't add more work – it replaces inefficient work with effective techniques. It's like upgrading from a blunt tool to a sharp, precise one.

Imagine approaching your next learning project with this toolkit. Whether it's a college course, a work certification, or a personal skill like learning guitar, you can design your learning process. For example, you begin a new job training by quickly surveying the training material (priming) and sketching a quick concept map. Each day, you take Cornell-style notes, then turn them into flashcards or summary questions. You meet with a colleague to explain the new procedures to each other (learning by teaching). Over the next month, you review your flashcards in Anki for a few minutes each morning, gradually spacing them out. When it's time for the official competency test, you feel ready – you've essentially been preparing in little bits all along, and performing self-checks that mirror the test. This approach could turn what might have been a stressful, last-minute slog into a calm demonstration of knowledge.

We also explored how these methods interconnect, creating a reinforcing cycle:

- **Priming and pre-testing** spark curiosity and guide your focus.

- **Layering and note-taking** give structure to your knowledge so you build a solid foundation before details.

- **Active recall (via self-quizzing, flashcards) and teaching** strengthen your memories and expose any illusions of knowing.

- **Mind mapping and interleaving** ensure you're making meaningful associations and can apply knowledge flexibly, not just in one context.

- **Spaced repetition** ties it all together over time, ensuring that what you learned remains accessible whenever you need it.

By mirroring these scientific principles in how this book was structured – starting with big problems, introducing core techniques, revisiting key ideas across chapters (for instance, recall how active recall popped up in almost every section as a critical component, reinforcing its importance) – the aim was not only to tell you about these methods but also to show them in action. If you found that concepts mentioned early on (like the forgetting curve or illusions of competence) reappeared later in new contexts, that's spaced reinforcement at work within these pages. The hope is that the reading itself has been a kind of educational experience, illustrating the methods as much as explaining them.

Key Takeaways Recap:

- **Don't just re-read – retrieve.** Testing yourself *is* studying. Use flashcards, practice problems, or simply recite what you know. This builds strong, retrievable memories and combats the familiarity trap.

- **Spread out your learning.** Plan multiple study sessions with time in between. A little every day beats a lot in one day. Use scheduling or apps to remind you. Cramming is a last resort, not a go-to strategy.

- **Structure information visually and hierarchically.** Before diving into details, understand the big picture (layer 1). Use mind maps or outlines to see connections. This makes learning meaningful (and meaningful material is remembered far better than random bits).

- **Use questions as your guides.** Convert notes into questions. Study by answering those. Also, constantly ask "why?" and "how?" – forcing yourself to explain or find answers reinforces depth of understanding and retention.

- **Teach and talk through material.** Even if your "student" is just your coffee mug on the table, articulate concepts out loud. This reveals what you truly know and what needs work – and you'll remember what you teach.

- **Mix practice, don't block.** Once you've got basics, alternate topics and problem types. It may feel harder but it's training your brain to apply the right knowledge in the right situation (just like a real test).

- **Take care of your brain.** Effective learning isn't just techniques, it's also avoiding burnout. Sleep (to consolidate memories), exercise (to improve focus and brain health), and taking breaks all enhance learning. Studying smarter often means you can study less and still do better – freeing time to rest.

- **Customize and reflect.** Everyone is a bit different. Use these methods as starting points, then notice what works best for you. Perhaps you find drawing diagrams especially helpful, or you notice you recall things much better when you explain them to a friend. Lean into those. The goal is to become a self-aware learner. After each exam or project, reflect: which techniques helped most? Where did you slip (maybe you crammed a section)? Adjust for next time.

Armed with these strategies, you can approach any subject with confidence that you have the tools to learn it effectively. This is incredibly empowering. Instead of saying "I'm not good at X," you'll say "I haven't learned X yet, but I know how to get there." Learning itself becomes a skill you continually hone – and one that pays dividends throughout life, well beyond school.

We live in a rapidly changing world where the ability to learn new skills and adapt knowledge is perhaps the most valuable skill of all. The methods in this book are not static tricks; they form a mindset of active, deliberate, and efficient learning. As science advances and more insights emerge (for instance, research into how technology like AI tutors or virtual reality might aid learning, or how certain brain training could complement these methods), you'll be able to incorporate those into this strong foundation.

In the "future of learning," traditional memorization will likely matter less (with information at our digital fingertips), but understanding, integrating, and using knowledge will matter even more. By practicing these strategies, you are essentially training to be an agile, lifelong learner – someone who can quickly get the gist of a new field, drill down to specifics, remember them, and apply them creatively.

Finally, remember that learning is a highly personal journey. **Embrace curiosity** – it's the fuel that makes all these techniques enjoyable rather than chores. When you layer knowledge, follow your interest: delve into the details that fascinate you, not just what's required. When you make a mind map, personalize it with images that mean something to you. When teaching, inject your passion or find an interesting angle to explain. These personal touches not only make learning fun, but also more effective (we remember what we care about).

In closing, the framework we've built together can transform your academic life and empower you beyond the classroom. It's a shift from passively ingesting information to actively conquering it – building knowledge the way an athlete builds strength, with technique and training. It's about studying smarter, to save time, reduce stress, and achieve mastery.

As you put these methods into practice, you'll likely experience a virtuous cycle: effective studying leads to better understanding and grades, which reduces stress and builds confidence, which in turn makes studying even more productive and perhaps even enjoyable. You might find yourself with more free time or the ability to take on additional interests, now that learning is more efficient. And when new challenges arise – be it a tough course, a certification for a promotion, or even self-teaching a hobby – you'll approach them not with intimidation, but with a strategist's mindset, equipped with the science of smart studying.

So, as you step forward, take this final encouragement: Apply these methods step by step. Start with one or two changes to your routine, then add more as you become comfortable. Each technique you adopt is like acquiring a new superpower for your mind. Over time, using them will feel natural – and the results will speak for themselves in your retention, your grades, and your confidence.

Your learning is now within your own control. You have the research-backed blueprint to master any subject and continue learning for life, long after any exam. Now, it's up to you to build, explore, and thrive with this knowledge. *Happy learning* – and remember: learn smarter, succeed easier, and never stop being curious. The world (and your brain) is yours to explore, one effective learning session at a time.

Bonus Chapter: Memory Palaces

A memory palace is a mental construct in which you place the things you want to remember along a well-known path or within a familiar location. In practice, it means associating pieces of information with specific physical locations in your mind. The technique relies on using memorized spatial relationships – the layout of a house, a route you know by heart, etc. – to organize and recall the information later. It's often called the method of loci ("loci" is Latin for places), the Journey Method, or the Roman Room technique. By mentally "walking" through your imagined space, you can retrieve the information you've stored at various spots.

Origins and History: The memory palace isn't a new hack – it's 2,500+ years old, dating back to ancient Greece. According to legend, the poet *Simonides of Ceos* discovered the method after a tragic banquet hall collapse. He survived and later recalled where each guest had been sitting to identify the bodies – realizing that location was the key to remembering who was where. This insight gave birth to the idea of storing memories in an imagined spatial layout. Ancient Greek and Roman orators widely practiced this technique. In an era with no teleprompters or paper notes, they would mentally place key points of their speeches in an imaginary building or along a familiar road. As they delivered the speech, they would walk through their "memory palace" in their mind, retrieving each point in order. For example, the Roman statesman Cicero reportedly used such vivid placeholders – one story describes him imagining a dead rat in a doorway to remind him to begin a speech with a scathing insult toward an enemy.

For over a thousand years, the memory palace (or "art of memory") was a staple of education and scholarship. Medieval monks, Renaissance scholars, and others used it to memorize vast amounts of knowledge – long before books were widely available. According to historian Frances Yates, this technique was in nearly every intellectual's toolbox until the invention of the printing press. Once books became an "external memory" technology, the use of memory palaces declined; people relied more on written information and less on training their minds. By the time journalist Joshua Foer explored memory palaces in his 2011 book Moonwalking with Einstein, the practice was kept alive mainly by memory enthusiasts and "memory athletes" who compete in memory championships.

Why Memory Palaces Work: The Cognitive Science Behind Spatial Memory

Why is a memory palace so effective for learning and retention? The power comes from aligning new information with how our brains naturally work. Human memory is fundamentally excellent at remembering places and visual images – skills that were crucial for survival (finding food, recognizing landmarks, recalling shelter locations). The method of loci essentially maps boring or abstract information onto our brain's instinct for spatial and visual memory, turning tough-to-remember data into something our minds handle with ease.

Several cognitive principles make memory palaces a superior memory technique. Our brains have dedicated neural circuitry for spatial navigation and memory (the hippocampus and related regions). We can effortlessly recall the layout of a childhood home or the route to the grocery store, even if we haven't been there in years. By tying information to specific locations in an imagined space, the memory palace engages this spatial memory system. As memory expert Boris Konrad explains, the strategy works by mapping "material that is really hard to remember" onto something the brain does extremely well – recalling imagery in specific locations. In essence, you are not increasing your brain's capacity, but using a different form of memory that already has a huge capacity. We have an almost unlimited mental warehouse for visual-spatial information, so a memory palace gives facts and figures a more natural home in your mind.

The method requires you to create vivid, and even bizarre, mental images for the information you want to remember, and place those images at your chosen loci (locations). This process is a form of elaborative encoding – you're encoding information (say, a concept or a term) by merging it with a rich image and context. The weirder or more emotionally striking the image, the better, because our brains tend to remember unusual things. (As the saying goes in memory training: "The more outlandish, the more outstanding" in your memory.) For example, memory champion Ed Cooke suggests that if you need to remember to buy cottage cheese, imagine supermodel Claudia Schiffer swimming in a tub of cottage cheese – an image so odd and vivid that it's hard to forget. By elaborating information into wild imagery, you make otherwise dull facts far more memorable. This works in line with dual coding theory – combining verbal information with visual imagery yields multiple mental cues, reinforcing memory traces.

A memory palace provides an organized framework for information. Instead of a disorganized list of 20 terms or facts, you have a structured journey with 20 specific stops. This spatial structuring inherently "chunks" the information into manageable pieces associated with each location. Chunking is known to enhance working memory and recall. The loci method also forces you to decide an order (e.g. the route through your house), which imposes a narrative or logical sequence on the material. When it's time to retrieve the information, you simply mentally walk through the path and the sequence unfolds naturally. The spatial cues help prevent items from blurring together because each lives in its own distinct spot. (Cognitive research has shown that memory interference is reduced when using distinct context cues – here each location serves as a unique context for each item.)

Constructing and using a memory palace is an active process. You're not passively reading notes – you're actively converting information into images, placing them, and later retrieving them by mentally touring your palace. This is essentially a form of active recall practice, which we know is the most powerful way to reinforce memory (as discussed in earlier chapters on retrieval practice). Each time you walk through your memory palace in your mind, you practice recalling the material without looking at notes, strengthening those neural connections. This active engagement also makes studying more fun and game-like, which can increase your focus and motivation. It's far more engaging to imagine crazy scenes in your living room than to repeat words on flashcards for the tenth time.

Interestingly, memory palaces work so well partly because they harness what you already know well (your mental map of a familiar place) to support new learning. By choosing a locus like your home or school, you leverage an existing strong memory as the scaffold for new information. This connects to the concept of priming – you're priming your brain with a contextual backdrop that is deeply ingrained, so any new information attached to it is easier to encode. The familiarity of the setting reduces the cognitive load of learning the new material, because your mind isn't struggling to also learn the context – the context is second nature. Essentially, you are linking new knowledge to prior knowledge (a key principle of learning) in a very literal way, by attaching it to a well-known place in your mind.

Brain imaging studies of memory experts provide compelling support for the above points. Remarkably, top "memory athletes" (people who compete in memory championships) don't have inherently superior brains – instead, they use different mental strategies. When researchers scanned memory champions' brains, they found that during memorization these individuals activate regions involved in spatial navigation and imagery much more than average people do. In other words, memory athletes are deliberately engaging their spatial memory networks (like the visual cortex and hippocampus) in unison to encode information – precisely what the memory palace technique encourages. Even more exciting, training ordinary people in the method of loci can alter their brain activity to resemble that of memory champions. In a 2017 study published in

Neuron, participants with no prior memory training were taught to use memory palaces daily for 6 weeks. The result: they massively improved their recall ability and their fMRI brain scans showed connectivity changes – after just 40 days, their brain's activation patterns looked much closer to those of world-class memory athletes. This illustrates that anyone can learn the memory palace technique and literally rewire their brain to be more efficient at memorization.

Scientific Research on Memory Palaces and Learning

The anecdotal feats of ancient orators and modern memory champions are impressive, but you might wonder: do memory palaces actually help everyday learners with real academic material? Scientific research says yes. Over the past few decades, numerous studies have tested the effectiveness of the method of loci for learning and retention, and the findings are consistently encouraging. Here we highlight some key research that demonstrates how powerful this technique can be:

As noted earlier, one landmark study trained ordinary adults on the memory palace technique and observed dramatic improvements. In this experiment, a group of volunteers practiced using a memory palace for 30 minutes a day over six weeks. When tested on recalling long lists of words, the memory palace group vastly outperformed two other groups (one that practiced short-term memory exercises without loci, and a no-training control group). After training, those using memory palaces could remember more than double the number of words compared to before , and significantly more than the other groups. Even more impressive, when researchers followed up four months later, the memory palace users still retained a much higher recall performance. This indicates that the technique doesn't just create a temporary boost – it helps form durable long-term memories. The same study also confirmed via brain scans that these individuals had developed memory networks similar to those of elite memorizers, suggesting a lasting change in how their brains stored information.

Memory palaces aren't only useful for memorizing random word lists or playing cards; they can also translate to better performance in academic subjects. For example, a 2014 study published in Advances in Physiology Education investigated using the method of loci to learn a medical topic (endocrinology, specifically insulin and diabetes). One group of medical students was taught to use a memory palace to organize and memorize key concepts, while another group learned via traditional lecture and study methods. When tested on the material, the students who used the memory palace scored significantly higher on their exams than those who relied on the usual study approach. This improvement was achieved without extra study time or spaced repetition – it was the memory technique itself that gave them an edge. The researchers concluded that method of loci can be a potent mnemonic to boost learning in complex subjects. Other studies in educational psychology similarly report that students who apply the loci method recall more facts and definitions, and do better on tests, than those who don't. The advantage is especially clear when dealing with information that benefits from being learned in a sequence or within a structured framework (think of processes in biology, events in history, steps in math proofs, etc.). By placing each step or element in a mental location, students create a storyline that's easier to follow and remember.

Another notable aspect of memory palaces is how broadly they can work. Research has shown that even populations who might struggle with complex strategies can learn this technique with some training. A large memory training trial with older adults (in the Advanced Cognitive Training for Independent and Vital Elderly study) included teaching the method of loci. Initially, almost none of the participants used a spatial strategy for memorization. But after training, up to 25% of the older adults adopted the memory palace technique for memorizing word lists, and those who did saw significant memory improvements – with effect sizes indicating substantially better recall. Impressively, their gains were maintained over follow-up sessions across five years. This dispelled the notion that memory palaces are "too difficult" or only for the young – seniors could use it effectively, proving our spatial memory remains a robust asset throughout life. Likewise, case studies of individuals with memory impairments or learning differences have found that loci techniques can sometimes help them leverage strengths (like visual memory) to compensate for weaknesses.

While not "laboratory studies," the achievements of modern memory competitors provide real-world evidence of what the method of loci makes possible. Competitive memorizers virtually all rely on memory palaces to perform astonishing feats: for instance, Clemens Mayer, a World Memory Champion, memorized 1,040 random digits in half an hour using a single 300-point journey through his house. Others have used the technique to memorize decks of cards in minutes or thousands of binary digits, demonstrating that with practice, a well-constructed memory palace can handle huge amounts of information. These feats underscore an encouraging point: the limitation in memorization is usually not our brain's capacity, but our strategy. By adopting the strategies of memory champions (adapted to our own learning needs), we can greatly expand our ability to retain information. In fact, memory contests were established in the 1990s largely to revive and showcase these ancient techniques, and their popularity has helped scientists discover just how trainable memory can be.

Decades of research and real-world evidence converge on the same conclusion – the memory palace technique is highly effective for enhancing memory and retention. It's not a gimmick or parlor trick; it's a skill that taps into fundamental memory mechanisms. From boosting exam performance in medical school to enabling record-breaking memories, memory palaces offer a proven way to encode information more durably. However, it's worth noting that memory palaces help you remember information – they don't replace understanding. In your studies, you'd use this tool to remember key facts, formulas, definitions, or sequences, but you still need to grasp the meaning and context (that's where the other layers of learning come in). When used appropriately, a memory palace can be the difference between struggling to recall basic details and having them at your mental fingertips.

Modern Applications: How Students and Professionals Use Memory Palaces

Beyond research settings, the memory palace has found many modern applications among students and professionals who need to absorb large amounts of information. Here are some ways this ancient technique is being applied today:

Perhaps the most common use is by students preparing for exams in fact-heavy subjects. For instance, medical and law students often have to memorize enormous volumes of material (anatomy terms, drug names, case law, etc.). Some create memory palaces to store and organize this information – like walking through the human body in their mind to place each anatomical structure at a location, or using a familiar neighborhood map to stash legal cases at different street corners. One medical education study guide noted that students who incorporated method of loci into their study routine outperformed their peers, especially when combined with other strategies like spaced repetition . Even if an entire curriculum can't feasibly go into one palace, students use multiple palaces or journeys for different topics. For example, a medical student might use one memory palace for pharmacology (e.g. envisioning a house where each room is a different drug category, filled with symbols of each medication) and another palace for physiology. Students report that this technique not only improves recall, but also makes studying more engaging – it turns learning into a creative imaginative exercise rather than rote memorization.

Memorizing vocabulary is another area where memory palaces shine. A modern language learner might choose a familiar walking route (say, around their hometown) and place an image for each new word at successive landmarks. If you're learning Spanish, you might put the word "la manzana" (apple) at your old school's gate by imagining a giant apple rolling through it. As you take a mental stroll, each location cues the foreign word you placed there. Many polyglots use this strategy to handle the large lexicons they must acquire. It's especially helpful for words that don't have an obvious mnemonic – by inventing a memorable scene and pinning it to a locus, even arbitrary terms can be recalled more easily. Professionals who work with multiple languages (translators, diplomats, etc.) have also used loci to keep technical vocabulary straight.

One classic application of memory palaces, harking back to Cicero, is for public speaking. Modern professionals, from TED talk speakers to lawyers delivering oral arguments, use the method to memorize the key points of their talks without notes. A common practice is to visualize the venue or an imaginary stage and place each section of the speech in a different spot. As you give the talk, you mentally move from spot to spot, retrieving the talking points in order. This technique not only ensures you don't forget what to say, but also can give your speech a more natural flow (since you're recalling ideas in a structured storyline instead of reading off a script). Famous anecdotes include people memorizing entire chapters or complex arguments by loci – for example, some trial lawyers have reportedly used a memory palace to remember every detail of a case file to argue in court. In business, executives might memorize key figures or strategy points for a pitch meeting using a palace, to impress stakeholders with a command of details without looking down at notes.

Outside of academics and work, memory palaces are a handy tool for everyday life tasks that involve memory. Want to memorize your to-do list or errands? Place each task along a route through your house (maybe imagine a broken lightbulb on your front step to remind you to buy bulbs, a stack of bills on the kitchen table to remind you to pay them, etc.). Learning a piece of music or lines for a play? Actors have been known to use loci to memorize scenes by assigning each line or cue to a different part of the stage or a path backstage. The technique is also popular among competitors in trivia, quiz bowls, or anyone who needs to retain lots of facts (like memorizing historical dates, sports statistics, or even digits of pi for fun). Some people even use memory palaces to store personal information they want to remember long-term – for instance, creating a "mental library" of favorite quotes, important phone numbers, or birthdays by placing them in different rooms. The flexibility of the method means you can adapt it to almost any scenario where you have multiple pieces of information to keep in mind.

A modern twist is using memory palaces in conjunction with digital tools. For example, some learners use virtual reality to create immersive memory palaces – VR allows you to construct and walk through a palace in a headset, which can enhance immersion. One study found that using a VR-generated environment as a memory palace led to about an 8.8% improvement in recall compared to using a desktop or imagining it, possibly because the richer sensory input (like feeling spatial presence) reinforced the memories. Even without VR, people have created software and apps to help build memory palaces or to share journeys for specific content (like an app that guides you through a memory palace for anatomy). While the classic technique needs nothing but your brain, these modern aids show how we can blend old and new: using technology to augment the ancient art of memory.

In all these applications, the memory palace serves as a mental filing system. It doesn't replace understanding or analytical learning, but it hugely boosts your ability to retain and retrieve the details that support that understanding. For students and professionals facing information overload, it's a way to efficiently store knowledge so that it's available when you need it – whether that's on a test, in a presentation, or just in conversation. As one memory champion put it, "Anyone can learn to improve their memory" with techniques like this you don't need a special brain, just a bit of creativity and practice. Next, let's see how you can integrate this powerful technique with the Layered Learning approach you've been following throughout this book.

Integrating Memory Palaces with Priming, Layering, and Revising

By now, you understand that Layered Learning involves building knowledge in stages (from basic to advanced) and using techniques like priming, active recall, and spaced repetition to maximize retention. The memory palace is a perfect advanced addition to this methodology – it doesn't replace those core strategies, but rather enhances them.

Here's how memory palaces can work alongside priming, layering, and revising:

Priming is about preparing your brain with an initial exposure or big-picture overview of the material before deep study. You can incorporate memory palaces at this stage by mentally mapping out your "palace" framework as you prime. For example, when you first skim a chapter (priming), note the major sections or categories – these might become the rooms or stops in your memory palace. The act of planning a palace leverages what you already know (a familiar location) to create curiosity and context for what you're about to learn. Even if you don't fill the palace with details yet, having a structured location scheme ready can make the upcoming information feel more organized. Priming is also about connecting new info to prior knowledge, and a memory palace does exactly that by tying new facts to a well-known place. Think of it this way: before diving into details, you decide where each type of information will "live" in your mind. This gives your brain a kind of roadmap, reducing cognitive load when you later learn specifics. It's like knowing the floor plan of a museum before you go in – you have a sense of where to put each new "exhibit" you encounter.

The concept of layering is to learn in multiple passes, each time adding more depth. You can use a memory palace in a layered fashion too. On your first learning pass (Layer 1), focus on the core ideas or categories and place those in your palace. For instance, suppose you're learning world geography. In Layer 1, you might create a palace (say, a familiar street) and place just the names of countries along different houses on the street. Once you've got that basic structure memorized, you move to Layer 2: add a second piece of information for each location. Maybe now at each house (country) you add the capital city as an image beside the country name. Because you already firmly memorized the countries in order (Layer 1), attaching capitals (Layer 2) is easier – you're not overwhelming yourself at once, you're building on an existing scaffold. Next, Layer 3 could add another detail, like each country's population or a landmark, placed at the same locus. By the end, your memory palace contains multiple layers of information at each location, but you learned them gradually, which mirrors the progressive deepening strategy of layered learning. This approach prevents the overload that can happen if you try to stuff all details in at once. It ensures each layer of detail has a "hook" – the images from previous layers – to attach to. In effect, the memory palace can evolve with each study session: start simple, then enrich the imagery with more data. Many learners find that this layered palace method helps them retain complex, detail-rich information much better than a single cramming session would. You're repeatedly engaging with the material (good for memory) and each time making the palace more informative.

A memory palace is only useful if you revisit it – much like how spaced repetition is critical for long-term retention of any study material. Luckily, memory palaces make revising both effective and engaging. When you review, instead of rereading notes, you challenge yourself to walk through your palace from memory. This is active recall practice, which, as we know, strengthens memory. You can do quick mental walk-throughs anywhere – while showering, during a commute, etc., making it a convenient revision tool. Integrating this with spaced repetition is straightforward: schedule reviews of your memory palace at increasing intervals (after 1 day, 3 days, a week, two weeks, etc.). Each time, note if any locations' images have faded or if you struggled to recall a detail. Those spots indicate what you should reinforce (perhaps by sharpening the image or adding another mnemonic cue). Because the information is chunked by location, you might find you only forget specific bits and can refresh just those, rather than re-learning everything. The memory palace structure also excels for self-quizzing during revision. For example, you can jump to a random location in your mind and see if you recall what's there, or you could write down all the loci in order on paper and attempt to fill in the info from memory. These are essentially mock-retrieval tests, harnessing the palace you built. Moreover, if you've layered information in your palace, revisiting it naturally involves recalling earlier layers too, which inherently spaces out your review of the foundational concepts while you add new ones. Over time, maintaining your memory palaces with periodic walkthroughs will ensure that even months later, you can still vividly recall what you stored. This aligns with the spaced repetition principle from Chapter 13 – the palace doesn't replace spaced practice, but it gives you a powerful way to perform that practice. In fact, memory palaces were shown to help form memories that lasted 4+ months with minimal decay which dovetails perfectly with a well-spaced revision schedule.

In short, think of the memory palace as an overlay onto the layered learning framework: priming gives you the blueprint (and the palace uses something you already know – your prior knowledge of a place – to set that blueprint), layering lets you fill in the palace incrementally, and revising (spacing) solidifies the palace's contents in your long-term memory. Used together, these strategies address both understanding (through layering and active engagement) and memorization (through spatial mnemonics and repetition). The result is a comprehensive approach where you truly learn the material and can also recall details with ease.

Building Your Own Memory Palace: A Step-by-Step Example

To cement how this works, let's walk through a concrete example of creating and using a memory palace in a study scenario. Imagine you're a student in a history class, and you need to memorize the major events of the French Revolution for an upcoming exam. There's a lot of information (multiple events, dates, and figures), so this is a perfect opportunity to apply layered learning and a memory palace. Here's how you might do it:

1. Priming and Planning: First, you skim your history textbook chapter or a timeline of the French Revolution (priming the content). You identify, say, five key events you must remember in chronological order: (a) the Meeting of the Estates-General (1789), (b) the Storming of the Bastille (1789), (c) the Declaration of the Rights of Man (1789), (d) the Reign of Terror (1793-94), and (e) the rise of Napoleon (1799). Now, choose a familiar place that has at least five distinct locations you can mentally walk through – perhaps your childhood home. This will be your memory palace.

Plan five loci along a natural route in the house. For example: front porch, living room, kitchen, staircase, and your bedroom. Just by doing this, you've given your brain a structured framework (your house) to fit the new info into, aligning with priming. You might even mentally rehearse the route a couple of times so it's fresh and ready.

2. Layer 1 – Main Ideas: On your first detailed study pass, focus on understanding each event (read about what happened, why it's important). Now create a simple image for each event and place it at the corresponding locus in your memory palace:

Front Porch – Estates-General: Visualize a giant estate (mansion) standing on your porch, with three cartoon figures (representing the Three Estates: clergy, nobility, commoners) trying to get in the front door which is blocked. This exaggerated scene will remind you of the Meeting of the Estates-General. Maybe the door has the year "1789" painted on it, to encode the year.

Living Room – Bastille: In your living room, imagine a huge medieval castle (the Bastille) bursting open with fireworks – symbolizing the Storming of the Bastille. Perhaps a crowd of angry peasants (tiny figurines) are running out of the TV set (the "fortress"). Make it wild: envision them tearing up couch cushions as if they are "storming" the room. The absurdity ensures you won't forget it.

Kitchen – Rights of Man: On your kitchen counter, picture a large scroll or document (the Declaration of the Rights of Man) being used as a tablecloth. Maybe on the scroll you see bold words like "Rights" or an image of hands breaking chains (freedom). You could have figures like Thomas

Jefferson (who influenced it) sitting on the counter signing a paper. The kitchen context might remind you that this was a foundational document (like bread and butter of the Revolution ideals).

Staircase – Reign of Terror: On your stairs, imagine a guillotine at the top of the staircase! It's dramatic but memorable. Perhaps visualize a character like Robespierre at the top stair, cackling, while the guillotine blade drops watermelons (to keep it light but clear). Blood-red carpeting on the stairs can emphasize "Terror." This encapsulates the bloody Reign of Terror.

Bedroom – Rise of Napoleon: On your bed, picture Napoleon himself standing, but to exaggerate, make him very small (since Napoleon was famously short) yet being lifted up by a huge eagle (the symbol of empire) from your bed. He's putting on a crown. This bizarre image fixes the idea of Napoleon's rise to power (from general to Emperor in 1799) in your mind.

Now, take a moment to mentally walk through your house and see each scene. Front porch? You see the estates struggling at the door – Estates-General 1789. Living room? The exploding Bastille castle – Bastille 1789. And so on. You've now encoded the five events in order with vivid images (Layer 1). Test yourself: can you name each event and its year by just walking through the loci in your mind? If yes – great. If one is fuzzy, strengthen the image or the association (e.g. if you forgot the year, make that part of the image more obvious).

3. Layer 2 – Adding Details: Next, enrich each location with an additional layer of detail. Suppose you want to remember a key figure or a concept associated with each event:

At the front porch (Estates-General), add the detail that the Third Estate broke away to form the National Assembly. So, you might imagine those three figures on the porch, and the commoner character dramatically walking away from the other two and unfurling a banner that says "National Assembly." Now your porch scene has the main event and this extra detail.

In the living room (Bastille) scene, maybe add the detail that this event symbolized the fall of royal authority. Represent that by showing King Louis XVI in the living room corner, looking bewildered as his crown falls off his head when the Bastille explodes.

In the kitchen (Rights of Man), add that this declaration established principles of liberty and equality. You could have a scale (weighing scales) on the kitchen table balancing two objects (symbolizing equality), or have the words "Liberté, égalité" appear as neon signs on the kitchen wall.

On the staircase (Reign of Terror), maybe note the year range or the magnitude of executions. You could add a calendar on the wall showing 1793–1794 dripping red, or a ghostly crowd on the stairs to hint at the thousands who died.

In the bedroom (Napoleon), add that Napoleon crowned himself Emperor in 1804 (a later detail, but related). So perhaps beside mini-Napoleon on your bed, place a big crown and engrave "1804" on it, even though your timeline locus is 1799 – it reminds you of his eventual emperor title, tying up the outcome of his rise.

Now mentally walk through again and recall both the main event and the added details at each stop. You've effectively layered more knowledge onto the sturdy backbone images you created initially.

4. Reinforce with Active Recall (Revision): Over the next days, use spare minutes to rehearse this memory palace. With each recall session, try to do it without looking at notes. Picture walking up to your house, visualize the scene on the porch – recall the Estates-General, 1789, National Assembly. Then enter the living room, recall Bastille, 1789, king's authority collapsing, and so on. If you find you forget something (say you recall the image but blank on the exact name "Declaration of the Rights of Man"), then revisit that spot in your notes and tweak your image (maybe you need to imagine the actual text "Rights of Man" glowing on the scroll to stick better). Because the images are distinctive, usually you'll find you remember them with minimal repetition, but spaced review is key to moving the info into long-term memory. After a week, you might still recall everything perfectly in order – and if the exam comes a month later, a quick refresher walk through your palace will reload all those facts in your mind. Essentially, you've made a complex historical sequence as easy to remember as the layout of your own home.

This example shows how a memory palace can be used step-by-step in tandem with understanding the material. Notice that at each stage, we still engaged with meaning (you need to know what the Estates-General was to create a meaningful image). The memory palace didn't do the learning for you – you did the learning, but the palace greatly aided in organizing and locking in the details. Also note how layering was applied: first pass for basic events, second pass for details. You could add even more layers (say, a third pass to add outcomes of each event, or a key date if not already included). This systematic approach prevents cognitive overload and uses the strengths of both the left brain (logical sequencing) and right brain (visual creativity).

Your memory palace should be a place you know extremely well (your childhood home, school, favorite park, the route to work, etc.), so that you can navigate it effortlessly in your mind. It should have a distinct layout with separate loci. If locations feel too similar, your images might clash or cause confusion. Clear physical separation (different rooms, landmarks) helps your brain compartmentalize information.

The effectiveness of a memory palace hinges on the vividness of your mental images. Go for multi-sensory detail – colors, sounds, motion. The more exaggerated, strange, or even funny/grotesque the image, the more it will stick. Don't be afraid to use humor or absurdity (as we did with the guillotine on the staircase or Claudia Schiffer in cottage cheese). If an image is dull, you likely won't recall it later, so amp it up: make things larger than life, out of place, or interacting in crazy ways.

To avoid overload and interference, generally place one idea per locus (at least in the early stages of learning). A locus can be a room or a specific spot in a room, but don't cram too many distinct facts into the same mental location initially.

It's better to create a second memory palace for extra items than to overcrowd one. That said, layering additional details onto a locus is fine if they connect to the main image. In our example, Napoleon and the crown were connected in one locus. They form one combined image (Napoleon with a crown) rather than two disjointed images at the same spot.

Always travel through your palace in a consistent order (e.g., always clockwise around the house, or always north-to-south along your mental map). This establishes a reliable sequence for retrieval. It can help to number your loci in your mind or have a narrative for your journey ("first the porch, then enter living room, then kitchen..."). If you ever want to recall the list out of order, you can still jump to the locus of interest, but in practice, walking the fixed route is the foolproof way to ensure nothing is skipped. Logical grouping of information by palace can also help – e.g. use different floors of a building for different categories, or different rooms for different subtopics, so that related facts are stored in the same general vicinity.

Like any skill, using memory palaces gets better with practice. Start with something fun (memorize a short list or a few key points) to get the hang of it. As you build confidence, you can take on larger palaces. Some memory experts maintain dozens of palaces for different purposes (memory competitors might have 50+ palaces memorized. For general studying, you might not need that many, but having a few go-to palaces (say your house, your school, a walking route) gives flexibility to store different subjects. One caution: avoid reusing the exact same palace for overlapping information in a way that could confuse you. If you fill your childhood home with facts for your biology exam, don't use the same childhood home loci for a history exam next week – you might mix up the content. Either use a different place, or significantly vary the imagery. Some people can reuse palaces by thoroughly "clearing out" the old images after an exam, but at least while learning, distinct palaces for distinct topics is safest to prevent interference.

Remember that memory palaces work best in combination with other strategies. Use priming to decide on your loci and get context. Use mind mapping or note-taking to understand relationships (you can even convert a mind map's branches into a memory palace journey). Use active recall by practicing your palace retrieval. And use spaced repetition by revisiting your palaces over time. Think of the memory palace as an advanced extension of the layered learning technique – it adds a strong memorization layer to the comprehension layers you're already building. Also, don't hesitate to supplement your palace with traditional mnemonics if needed (e.g., maybe you still use an acronym for a list but visualize that acronym spelled out in your palace location). All these tools can coexist.

By following these best practices, you'll avoid common pitfalls (like dull images or confusing locations) and make your memory palaces truly effective. It might feel a bit strange at first to assign wild imagery to serious study material, but as countless learners and memory masters have discovered, it works. With a bit of creativity, even the driest fact can become a memorable scene in your imagination.

The memory palace technique shows us just how adaptable and powerful the human memory can be when we use it the way it was designed – visually and spatially. What began in ancient Greece as a way for bards and orators to remember their lines can today complement cutting-edge educational strategies. Within the Layered Learning methodology, memory palaces serve as a bridge between acquiring knowledge and remembering it long-term. They ensure that the effort you put into understanding (through priming and layering) isn't lost to forgetfulness. Instead, your knowledge is actively encoded in a durable form, ready to be retrieved when you need it.

Importantly, using memory palaces can make learning more enjoyable. Studying becomes a more creative, game-like process of imagination. This not only boosts retention but can also reduce study stress and burnout – suddenly, reviewing for an exam might involve a fanciful stroll through your "mental mansion" of knowledge rather than a grueling cram session. It's a reminder that learning is as much an art as it is a science.

As you continue to refine your study skills, consider this advanced technique as a secret weapon. Whether you're a student aiming for top grades, a professional picking up new skills, or a lifelong learner, memory palaces can help you remember more, for longer. They exemplify the balance of science and practical application: grounded in cognitive research and proven through experience. In embracing the memory palace, you're tapping into a timeless learning strategy and bringing it into the modern age – truly an ancient technique for modern learning mastery.

Thank you for reading *Layered Learning: Master Any Subject Faster, Crush Every Exam, and Retain Information Forever*! I hope that you've gained just as much value out of this information as I have, and that you are able to utilize the techniques in this book to master your studies. If you enjoyed this book, please be on the lookout for others that I may end up writing. I have already begun journaling and brainstorming a book on the way mind mapping and memory palaces can be used together in interesting ways. Again, thank you!

Printed in Dunstable, United Kingdom